ERIC OWEN MOSS 2

E E

Never to keep, really; never the same for the clock-
        shaped, corpse-caped schemer to ports.
There—their's—never.

Sennets from the Tortuquise
— Moss Herbert

BUILDINGS AND PROJECTS 2

ERIC OWEN MOSS

INTRODUCTION BY
ANTHONY VIDLER

COMPILED BY
BRAD COLLINS

RIZZOLI
NEW YORK

First published in the United States of America in 1996
Rizzoli International Publications, Inc.
300 Park Avenue South, New York, NY 10010

Library of Congress Cataloging-in-Publication Data
Moss, Eric Owen, 1943–
Eric Owen Moss, buildings and projects 2/
introduction by Anthony Vidler
p. cm.
Includes bibliographical references.
ISBN 0-8478-1909-4 – ISBN 0-8478-1910-8 (pbk.)
I. Moss, Eric Owen, 1943– –Themes, motives.
2. Architecture, Modern–20th century–United States–Themes, motives.
I. Title.
NA737.M73A4 1991   91-52885
720'.92–dc20   CIP

Printed and bound in Hong Kong

DESIGNED AND
COMPOSED BY
Group C Inc
NEW HAVEN (BC, CK, FS, EZ)
EDITED BY
BRAD COLLINS AND ELIZABETH ZIMMERMANN

THE BAROQUE EFFECT

Anthony Vidler

THE EARLIER WORK INVESTIGATED OVERLAPPING GEOMETRIC ENTITIES. THEN INTERIOR SPACE—
LAWSON/WESTEN. NOW IT'S THE SPACE BETWEEN INSIDE AND OUTSIDE, WHERE GEOMETRIES DANCE.
THE SPACE IN-BETWEEN IS FLEXING—INSIDE OF THE OUTSIDE AND THE OUTSIDE OF THE INSIDE.
—ERIC OWEN MOSS

Rejecting the ascription "jeweler of junk" bestowed by Philip Johnson in his preface to the first volume of this work (Rizzoli, 1991), and distancing himself from a too-pervasive deconstruction, Eric Owen Moss now stakes out a ground originally prepared by modernist theory and practice—space—as a starting-point for his own increasingly complex geometrical explorations. In the context of postmodernism and deconstruction, this claimed filiation might have a nostalgic, even retro, air—reminiscent of Bruno Zevi, Christian Norberg-Schulz, postwar smugness, and comfortable fifties shoes—if it were not so elegant in its tactical simplicity. Space, geometry, structure: the three themes that resonate through this iteration bypass entirely almost every question of style and cutting-edge theory of the last decades, referring instead to the supposed fundamentals of architecture, especially modern architecture. For the idea of space and the image of modernism have been intimately connected since the turn of the century, in historical theory as in architectural practice. If the aesthetic psychology and sociology of Theodor Lipps and Georg Simmel, and the historical studies of August Schmarsow and Paul Frankl, confirmed the essential role of space in the analysis of architectural history—"space, protagonist of architecture"[1] as Bruno Zevi put it in 1948—the polemics of Le Corbusier and Mies van der Rohe and their followers dramatically attested to its essential place in a truly modern architecture.

There has been, of course, no lack of contenders for a "return" to, or a "continuity" with, modernism in the last quarter of a century: From late modernists like Richard Meier and endless avant-gardists like Peter Eisenman to those more or less self-consciously implicated in deconstruction has come the persistent refrain of a modernist century that refuses to hide beneath the excesses of postmodern eclecticism. But in the case of Moss, the need to distinguish himself from neomodernist architects on the one hand and expressionist deconstructionists on the other has generated a different note, one that perhaps signals a slight shift in the framing of fin-de-siècle apologetics.

For Moss assays his critical return to the basics of modernity in relation to the principles of space and structure expounded in that by now canonical text, Siegfried Giedion's *Space, Time and Architecture,* published in 1941. Not, of course, that we are expected to read Giedion as trustingly as before; a half-century of counter-modernist critique and debased modern practice has given the lie to space, geometry, and structure as virtues in themselves, and Giedion's structural and spatial determinism seem quaintly out of place in a poststructuralist universe. Rather, Moss explicitly sets up Giedion as a structural reductionist who left out the most important architectural ingredient of all in neglecting the content, whether spiritual or artistic.

Implicitly, *Space, Time and Architecture*'s attempt to trace the "growth of a new tradition" sets up the coordinates for Moss's retelling of an old story. We are, by inference at least, asked to place Moss's self-constructed itinerary from geometrical entities and western interiority to his more recent experimentation with inside and outside in the context of the strong narratives of Giedion's historicism. And certainly, Moss provides an account that bears some resemblance to Giedion's own biography of modernism, from the Renaissance through the baroque, to the structural innovations of the nineteenth century, and thence to the "new space-time synthesis." But, the significant difference is that, where Giedion's book attempted to establish its thesis firmly on the assumed congruence of modernism and historical progress, Moss is forced to avoid any simplistic reduction of terms like structure and space that seem to evince the very opposite of stability. Moss's space, like his geometry, is conceived as shifting, flexing, and jumping, described in gerundive terms that would have delighted the romantics of the early nineteenth century and given him a place among the organicists of architecture.

But the parallels with Giedion go further and perhaps throw a new light on the particular character of Moss's work from the outset—his insistence on the distortion, reformulation, and mutation of pure geometries (the circle, the cube, the cone) that has been generally uncharacteristic of recent radical attempts to deconstruct tradition (whether by Frank Gehry or Coop Himmelblau). If, for a moment, we were to escape the theoretical prejudices of the present, we might find it instructive to read Moss's oeuvre not in the light of junk or constructivism but as an extended and intensely worked meditation on the formal predilections and pathological insights of Giedion and his generation—Emil Kaufmann, for example, or Hans Sedlmayr. We might thus be able to construe a kind of formal evolution, as these historicists would have put it, from the rational cylindrical and conical geometries of Moss's PIN BALL HOUSE and the FUN HOUSE, to the more broken and shattered forms of the 708 HOUSE, the PETAL HOUSE, and HOUSES X AND Y, to the narrative architecture parlante of the RESERVOIR HOUSE, to the overlapping geometries of the YOKO UEHARA HOUSE. These geometries would then be the starting point for more public work, such as the LOWER EAST SIDE HOUSING FOR THE INDIGENT PAVILION, the ESCONDIDO CIVIC CENTER, and the TOKYO OPERA HOUSE. This would be the moment where all of these formal experiments found an ideal home, so to speak, in what has become Moss's own little utopian community, the Frederick Smith developments in Culver City.

In such an imaginary history we would be presented not with deconstruction, and certainly not postmodernism, or even modernism as it was adumbrated by the "masters" of the 1920s and 1930s. Moss would be seen to be reflecting on an even more foundational route—that described in Kaufmann's book of 1933, *Von Ledoux bis Le Corbusier.* In this little book, published in Vienna on the eve of the Nazi putsch in Berlin and just before Kaufmann's own exile, Kaufmann draws a direct connection between form (independent, rational) and the rise of bourgeois society (freedom of the individual, social democracy) to support an argument that intriguingly joins the generation of the 1730s (Ledoux, Boullée, Lequeu) to that of the 1930s (Le Corbusier, Walter Gropius), with Ledoux and Le Corbusier as the heroes. A similar argument, with different heroes and villains, was to be made by Giedion and Sedlmayr.

Whether or not Moss's own history refers self-consciously to such obviously oversimplified historical genealogies, the implied reference to the formal and spatial origins of modernism is nevertheless revealing on two counts. First, it definitively separates Moss from the rationalism of the neorationalists and from the pastiche-rationalism of the postmodernists, neither of which was fundamentally concerned with geometry as the basis of architectural invention. Second, it puts him in the context of an alternative modernism, as compared to that of the functionalists and structural determinists, one represented, interestingly enough, by the last hero cited by Kaufmann—Richard Neutra, whose statement from California rings hauntingly from the last page of *Von Ledoux bis Le Corbusier* and seems tellingly to anticipate Moss's critique of Giedion's structural determinism: "It is a long way from the plastic formalism of the Greek world to the swelling facades of the baroque, but this route is not illogical, it always traverses, so to speak, the same region: that of a certain spiritual attitude towards architectural creation."[2] And the form of this spirituality was, in Neutra's and Kaufmann's terms, geometrical, dominated by the predilection for simple forms.

Here, of course, we are presented with a tantalizing nexus of further imaginary associations. It is tempting, for example, to raise the possibility of a California modernism, forged by Neutra and now transformed and permutated a half-century later. This might well be an exilic practice, driven to geometry in its search for stability in movement. We might also, paradoxically, find ourselves crossing paths with Philip Johnson in the 1930s and 1940s, intersecting his very different modern trajectory at the moment when Kaufmann himself introduced Johnson to the forms of Ledoux in his first Harvard seance of 1943.

Johnson himself, in his concise preface to *Eric Owen Moss: Buildings and Projects* (1991), preferred a genealogy for the work that operated by generation: the fathers (Mies, Corbusier et al.); the emulators and first sons (Johnson et al.); the "kids" (Gehry, Eisenman et al.); and the children of the "kids" (Eric Owen Moss, Morphosis et al.). And with a twist of the family tree that shifted the responsibility for these last children away from the grandfathers and fathers to another paternity altogether (Sullivan through Scarpa), Johnson neatly proclaimed them both orphans and bastards, characterized by their transgression against modernist spatial planning and their fundamentally ornamental preoccupation. In this way, Johnson was able to characterize Moss as the "jeweler of junk," at once complimenting his skill (as a diamond peddler?) and implying the marginality of his practice: the jeweler/peddler, at home in the wasteland of LA, but denied the spatial pedigree of truly western architecture.

Inevitably, Johnson was following the modernist ploy of affirming the authenticity of space against the inauthenticity of ornament, which was, if not crime, at least superfluity, and therefore lesser. From Giedion to Henry-Russell Hitchcock, Zevi, and Johnson himself, space has been the litmus test of true architecture in its long history from volumetric solidity to ineffable fluidity—as Giedion put it, from rock temple to Le Corbusier, or, in Johnson's terms, from Greece to Mies. And, as the Greco-Roman cultural tradition during the period of nineteenth-century national romanticism in Germany, England, and France had been welded to Gothic political roots, so space was joined to the morality of structure (whether Puginesque or Choisyesque) that determined precisely the limits of the ornamental. Space and structure, then, in turn were endowed with socially ethical ends in order to construct the well-known ideological complex known as morality in architecture. In this context, Johnson's description of a new generation's work as ornamental and not spatial was hardly innocent.

At the same time, however, and in the context of Moss's own assertion of his spatial identity, one would have to admit, with Johnson, that if space were indeed a central characteristic of Moss's work, it would certainly not be the clear, open, and ineffable space of modernism. Structural complexity, apparently unnecessary and seemingly gratuitous if not ironically redundant, joined to geometrical combinations and hybrid forms, render space difficult to identify, at least in the traditional ways. To see space at work here, one would have to reformulate its very qualities, its roles, even its representa—tional modes.

Yet there is a way in which we might see Moss's spatial complexities in a direct lineage from modernism, especially Giedion's formulation of modernist space as distinctively cubist in nature. As Giedion summarized it in his description of Le Corbusier's Maison Savoie [Villa Savoye],

> It is impossible to comprehend the Savoie house by a view from a single point; quite literally, it is a construction in space-time. The body of the house has been hollowed out in every direction: from above and below, within and without. A cross section at any point shows inner and outer space penetrating each other inextricably.[3]

Such interpenetration, or overlapping, as he calls it elsewhere, first evident in cubism and later adopted by architecture, was for Giedion the sign of modernity. As he noted of Gropius's *Totaltheater* project, "the new space conceptions" were represented by cubism's rejection of a "fixed point for every perspective" and by its presentation of a "many-sided spectacle."[4]

The sources of this kind of spatial ambiguity were, for Giedion and his immediate predecessors, embedded in the baroque and its complex questioning of Renaissance perspectival stability and realist representation. The combination of perspectival multiplicity and illusion that these historians found in Borromini and Guarini seemed, in retrospect, to prefigure cubism. When joined to the spatial inter-penetration exhibited in the engineered structures of the late nineteenth century, the potential of the baroque was turned into constructive possibility: "this possibility was latent in the skeleton system of construction, but the skeleton had to be used as Le Corbusier uses it," concluded Giedion, "in the service of a new conception of space." [5]

In this model of spatial history, the role played by structure became pivotal; Giedion's pairing of Borromini's lantern of Sant'Ivo with Tatlin's project for a Monument to the Third International has itself become a commonplace of architectural history, as has his analysis of Guarini's cupola of San Lorenzo. It remained only for modern construction methods to overcome these limits and for modern architects to imagine modern space, and the equation *spatial imagination* + *structural invention* = *progress* would be confirmed.

Such a myth of a "modern" baroque has exhibited remarkable persistence through many permu-tations in the twentieth century ever since Heinrich Wölfflin, in 1888, remarked on the powerful affinity between his epoch and that of the baroque.[6] At once celebrating the structural inventiveness and spatial complexities of a baroque that seemed protomodernist and decrying the evident dissolution of the classic, harmonious space established by Renaissance humanism, this myth of the baroque has had a dual and often intersecting history. For Giedion, as we have seen, the baroque was triumphant and projective; for others, including Wölfflin and Walter Benjamin (as well as his more recent postmodern exegetes), the baroque represented an end to an architecture of stability and perfection. Against what Benjamin saw as the balance between excess and lack achieved by Renaissance harmony, the baroque signaled the dissolution of all forms and boundaries; its penchant for spatial illusion and dramatic lighting effects led to the transgression of the natural limits of architecture.[7] For Benjamin, writing in the 1920s, the analogy was more poignant still, joining two periods of decadence by means of a symp-tomatic analysis of forms in tumult, disrupted forms that were emblematic of the conflictive forces of their respective epochs. As with many myths surrounding the emergence of modernism, the baroque effect was seen in terms of light and dark, rather as modernity itself was construed as poised between reason and the abyss of expres-sionist exaggeration.

It is in relation to this double tradition that Moss's geometrical work begins to take on a certain significance beyond its merely incidental, and perhaps accidental, filiations to the more general historiography of modernism. For there is much evidence in Moss's projects that a mod-ern baroque of some kind is at work, at the level of overt formal similarities as well as theoretical inference. At the visual level alone, many paral-lels would fascinate a latter-day Giedion: she might choose, for example, to pair the dome of San Lorenzo with the Culver City conference room, or the vault to the GARY GROUP entrance lobby, or even the elliptical insertions in the YOKO UEHARA HOUSE. There are comparisons, no doubt, to be drawn between Gropius's *Totaltheater* project and the INCE THEATER in the notion of a many-sided spectacle. The com-plex reworkings of spherical geometry in, say, the ARONOFF HOUSE, the LAWSON/WESTEN HOUSE, and, in more public modes, in the R3 THEATER, the PLAZA VIEJA, or the CONTEMPORARY ART CENTER, recall the spherical projects of Ledoux,

Boullée, and their contemporaries, with a suitably baroque twist. Equally, the complex, eroded, lean-ing, and warped planes and facades of SAMITAUR and STEALTH or the facades of the GARY GROUP, might be seen in relation to the undulating and pressured walls of Borromini and Guarini. At an urban level, and according to the formal comparisons deployed by Giedion himself, we might finally look to the bridge infrastructure of SPARCITY as it moves serpentining through east Culver City, and to the eighteenth-century precedents for such serpentine moves in John Nash's terraces in Bath, themselves cited by Giedion as the origins of Corbusian urban planning.

In each case structure is put in play to articulate geometry, which in turn pushes the bound-aries of a succession of intersecting and overlapping spatial entities, leading to the delineation of a complex warped space, ambiguously balanced between "inside" and "outside." Space itself is "folded" somewhat in the manner described by Gilles Deleuze in his explication of Leibniz's elaboration of baroque mathematics, a mathematics of variability, inflection, and tangent curves.[8]

Here, however, we have reached the limits of a baroque that is legitimately filiated to any recognizable modernism, whether cubist or purist. By contrast, we are precipitated into a world of half-ruins and fragments, shattered wholes and disseminated entities, of a violence expressed through and even against geometry. Such a topos, indeed, seems seems to echo that other, negative, baroque, identified throughout the modern period as the sign of ending, of melancholy, and of the empty frames of allegorical rhetoric. Whether or not one chooses to follow this trail of analogy to the present fin de siècle and its formal and social disruptions, it is clear that those of Moss, at least, cannot be read without reference to this alternative pathology, one that admits the incongruity, if not the impossibility, of artistic achievement conceived according to laws of harmony and autonomy, and, for better or worse, understands a perpetually unfixed manner of expression as the representation of a work that attempts to infuse new life, perforce with violence, into the shells of forsaken dwellings, sites, and landscapes.

In the context of this admittedly imaginary plot, where baroque refers more to modernist fan-tasies of spatial explosion than to any seventeenth-century historical condition, Moss's recent work seems positioned at the intersection of Giedion's progressive hope and Benjamin's melancholic pathology. In its formal experimentation and its exploration of spatial ambiguity, not to speak of its evident commitment to a renewed public realm, it continues, albeit with conscious dislocation, a long modernist tradition; in its assertion of a narrative comprised of allegorically redolent fragments, it fittingly represents a new fin-de-siècle condition where the utopian symbols of modernity have necessarily lost their former allure.

Los Angeles, 1995

NOTES

1 Bruno Zevi, *Saper vedere l'architettura. Saggio sull'interpretazione spaziale dell'architettura* (Milan: Einaudi, 1948), 21.

2 This citation was taken by Kaufmann from Richard Neutra's *Wie baut Amerika?* (Stuttgart: J. Hoffman, 1927), 69.

3 Siegfried Giedion, *Space, Time and Architecture: The Growth of a New Tradition* (Cambridge: The Harvard University Press, 1941), 416.

4 Ibid., 405.

5 Ibid., 416.

6 See Heinrich Wölfflin, *Renaissance and Baroque*, translated by K. Simon, introduction by Peter Murray (Ithaca, NY: Cornell University Press, 1966). This sentiment was echoed in turn by Alois Riegl, Frankl, Giedion, and Walter Benjamin in the first half of the century, and more recently by Zevi, Paolo Portoghesi, Robert Venturi, and, among other critics, Gilles Deleuze and Jacques Lacan.

7 See Walter Benjamin, *The Origin of German Tragic Drama*, translated by John Osborne (London: Verso, 1985).

8 Gilles Deleuze, *The Fold: Leibniz and the Baroque*, foreword and translation by Tom Conley (Minneapolis: University of Minnesota Press, 1993), 19.

Gravity Is Only Temporary

Eric Owen Moss

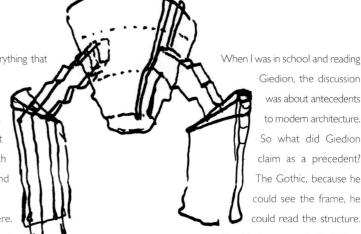

Gravity is only temporary. Everything that stands, falls. But everything that falls gets back up again (in one form or another).

It occurs to me that the question of instability is related to an unsteady psychological state in the architect and in the culture. Architecture should look at that condition and say something about it—that it exists, that it's difficult, and that it would be intelligent both to put it down and to suggest a way one might learn from it and move on.

Architecture has to move. It has to be pulled somewhere. Otherwise all you've got is the deconstruction discussion—which is not where this work goes. Deconstruction wallows, massaging its own nihilism. It's a cynical nihilistic promotion, and nihilism is too desperate to be promotion.

I want to build instability, then obviate it. As soon as I insist that this is absolutely the way, I'm prepared to show myself another vantage point. Multiple vantage points. Come after the truth through contradiction.

The truth is vibrating. It's not sitting there to be picked up. To record the truth, you have to record the vibration: a perpetual movement. But to reform that as architecture you have to distill it, freeze it. And if you freeze it, you've lost the reverberation. So you freeze it lots of times to depict the extent to which it reverberates, but it doesn't reverberate infinitely—multiple vantage points and limits.

So this is not relativism. It's absolute relativity. I would like to call it that as opposed to relative-relativity. If it's relative-relativity you can never stand anywhere and say anything because somebody can always say, "On what basis do you say it's all relative?" That's an absolute in a framework that won't tolerate any absolutes. So relative and absolute together would be the construct. Absolute-absolute is inflexible. Relative-relativity is nowhere. Absolute-relativity is malleable, but not infinitely so.

Relativism seems to be a way of avoiding anything that's unequivocal—you can always say the opposite. I want the building to deliver oppositions but not infinite opposition; I want it to be a building that wouldn't swallow distinctions, but would clarify that the interrelationship of contradicting pulls remains tense. The resolution isn't a homogeneous synthesis. It's a heterogeneous resolution. Architecture as intentional oxymoron. Architecture as dialectical lyric, and the dialectic is resolved lyrically, not intellectually.

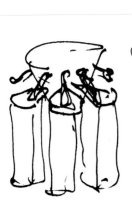

When I was in school and reading Giedion, the discussion was about antecedents to modern architecture. So what did Giedion claim as a precedent? The Gothic, because he could see the frame, he could read the structure. Empirical cause and effect—they correlate. But what about big cause, little effect? Or little cause, big effect? Those are real, too. The Gothic had a premise, and it wasn't Giedion's. The Gothic means is technique. But the means is directed by the end—the delivery of God as light and space. How to build God? Giedion dropped God and discussed the flying buttress. He assumed the means was the end. Or, he assumed the discussion of God was antiquated and only the structural form-language of space was relevant. So technique became means and end. Synonymous. Very contemporary. A naive way of looking at technique. No end except technique, now a tired sensibility. Nothing except the machine metaphor—and that can't drive architecture very far.

I'm arguing that the content underneath what you see precipitates what you see. Underneath technique gives me a basis for making all kinds of decisions about what buildings should look like. Underneath doesn't make all those decisions. Where some of those decisions come from, I'm not certain. But in thinking about the process in the abstract, it's important to get under the idealization of the technical prowess, or the alleged technical prowess, of contemporary culture.

Then there's the socially responsible, decency advocacy: design by the (self)righteous. Well, there's also a hell of a lot of vanity in being decent. Which doesn't preclude the fact that it's nice to be nice. But what's underneath being nice? Underneath you might meet a lot of things that aren't so nice.

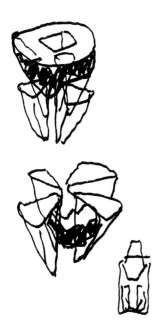

There's always a concern for the object as abstract. Not merely space, but more maniacal than that. What can I do to the space that compresses or stretches it? I hate Ezra Pound. He's diabolical in a lot of ways, and hasn't been given his due in that regard. But he made the remark, "Make it new," and in some ways he may have. Life is about discovering. The world doesn't stay the same. Altering the world is possible, and I know that the process of discovering is redemptive. This architecture is about discovery. It insists that the world can be other than it is.

Hedonistic details are of less interest now; maybe a particular piece is OK–the door to LAWSON/WESTEN. Things big are made out of things small. You have to put the small things together. The question is, how are the small things put together, or does putting the small things together to make the big thing supersede the aspiration of the big thing? The answer is no. Detail is ancillary. Distracting.

I have to say that that was a terribly misinformed exegesis…the Jeweler of Junk. It's like the German television crew that came the other day and said, why are you doing all of this whips and chains stuff? It was never about that.

The spatial language is deeper than the hedonism of detail, however seductive. Dig, follow your nose, follow your instincts to the heart of the problem, and do not turn your head. Although it's seductive, the west wall of the GARY GROUP turned my head from the essential job of the architecture. I won't turn my head anymore.

I'm using the fundamental instrument, geometry. So much energy has been spent in the last twenty years not dealing with space, with volume, with the core concern of architecture. The subject is stretching space—architecture's perpetual prospect. How to do that?

Should the underlying mechanisms for ordering remain invisible? Should a preexisting, theoretical sphere be as legible as its punched-up actuality? That's an open question for me, whether what I do underneath ought to be intelligible to people who use and inquire about what they see. To what extent is the theorizing of the building part of the visible understanding of the building? Does the building stand separate from the process of developing or deriving? Is the building what it is, or is how it came to be? Is it the end, or the sequence of development? I put the building out there and people pick it up and misunderstand it, sometimes in imaginative ways. But they never pick it up exactly the way I put it down. I think that has to do with seeing and what precedes seeing—how you look at something and understand it, or not, as a consequence of either what you bring to it or what it can teach you: a way of learning to think that you don't yet know. My buildings aspire to teach you to think in a different way, meaning the prospect exists that you would think again about how you think.

The earlier work investigated overlapping geometric entities. Then interior space—Lawson/Westen. Now it's the space between inside and outside, where geometries dance. The space in-between is flexing—inside of the outside and the outside of the inside.

It's not spatial strangeness I'm after, it is the tension between the understandable and the un-understandable. The experience seems strange because it isn't immediately grasped. It's not strange. That's not what I'm about, though sometimes people characterize the work that way.

My work is an attempt to build, very incisively, the effort to understand—a very intense effort notwithstanding the fact that it's not likely to be successful (but it might be). It's a perpetual maybe: that the space could become intelligible or graspable or manageable exists solely as a prospect. Architecture is life is space—the form-language of space. Architecture can't talk. It's not so much a translation from spoken language to space; it's this transmutated conversation from conceptual content to space in architecture, the way Goya would speak in paint or Kafka in words. Architecture's form-language makes space.

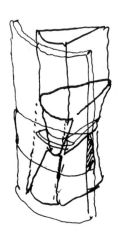

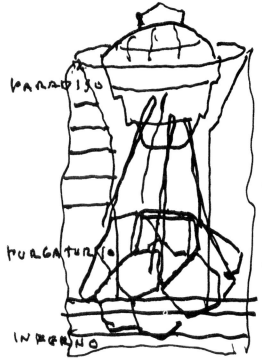

PARADISO

PURGATORIO

INFERNO

Sometimes I can see pivot points or jumps. The PETAL HOUSE was a jump. The Gary Group was a leap. It was the first time I raised the issue of truth as a contradiction, what I'm calling balance or the problem of balance: balance looking for imbalance, imbalance looking for balance. What is precarious and most fragile is also the most precious, but what's most fragile is also the least durable. And human instinct is to take whatever is precious and try to make it durable. Hold on and give it a future. The Gary Group sustains the fragile. Buildings can do that. Buildings can freeze the poignant in a way that a human institution can't.

At certain times it works; you hit it. The Gary Group's tilting front wall could be accounted for by a conventional structuralist exegesis: what holds what, what cause, what effect. Very intentionally I tried to abrogate or confuse that argument, but not totally lose it, so that a tiny cause might have an enormous effect. Or an enormous cause might have almost no effect, which is a way of disowning the empirical pedigree I inherited. The wall of the Gary Group touched on that. It leans, but is its inclination to fall or to straighten up?

An exegesis for the Gary Group conference room is a little harder. It's still in the category of a hybridization of pieces one could recognize singly, but there are so many of them. I want to say that they are piled on one another, but they're not piled; they're assembled carefully. Although carefully doesn't necessarily mean delicately. Incisively. Incisive force. The ARONOFF HOUSE is also force. Power. There is another motivation underneath, a will to power, manifest in the force of the architecture. In Lawson/Westen it's the big space: dichotomies, oppositions. Intellectually, it's multiple vantage points. Then the emotive power of the space lifts you over the differences, resolves the contradictions at the next level. But it doesn't dissolve the contradictions. You arrive at a place where the contentious parts are never one literally, but become one figuratively in their power to make the thing what it is lyrically. Architecture as dialectical unity. Everything else is digression.

New Haven, 1995

BOX

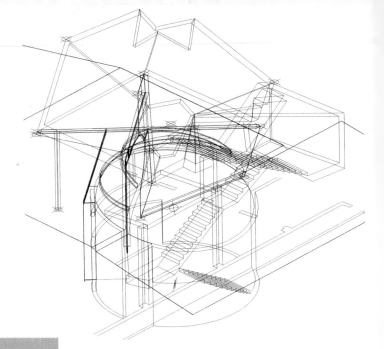

SOMETIMES CARTESIAN DOESN'T CLARIF

IT OBSCURES.

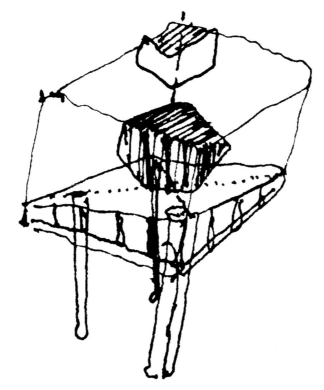

The Box is only nominally so. This almost-box rolls on a theoretical sphere, disconnected from the horizontal and vertical.

Inside the box is a flat floor. That horizontal plane might have brought its own spatial arguments, but it didn't have the capacity to do so. The floor can't resist the shape in which it sits.

The Box is broken and repaired. Done away with and brought back, redemptive and optimistic; wants to resolve. The Box takes an aesthetic position, a political position, a social position. It's a building. But it isn't about utility. Anyone who has walked through a cemetery could go in the Box and come to understand the aspirations of the building. Everybody's in the same leaky boat. Take the Box and plug the leak.

The Box is black. It's a mausoleum, related to my father, very traditional. Wolf Prix called it a synagogue. But the color is not simply black. You can't name it. The color is related to death, but it's equivocal. The color is everywhere, relentlessly the color that is not a color. I like the possibility that somebody could look and experience, but wouldn't have a label. And it's very tactile—that black stuff. Cut a hole through the color. Black exterior. Black jam. Black head. Black sill. When you get to the inside wall it's the same black that's not black.

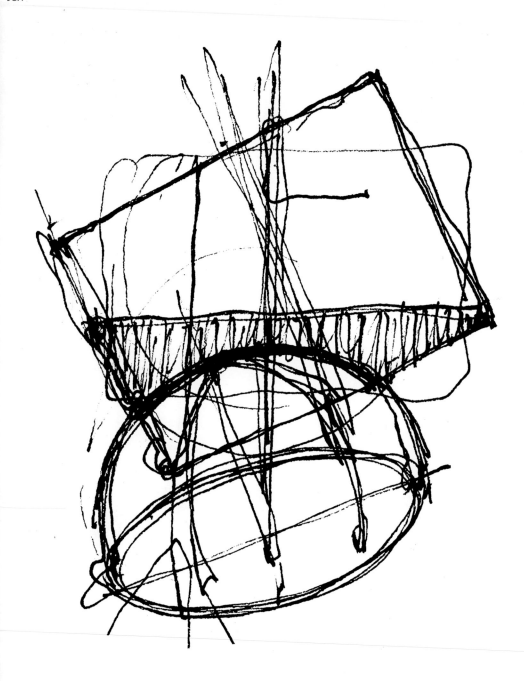

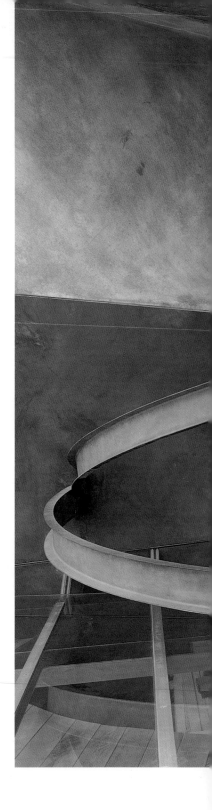

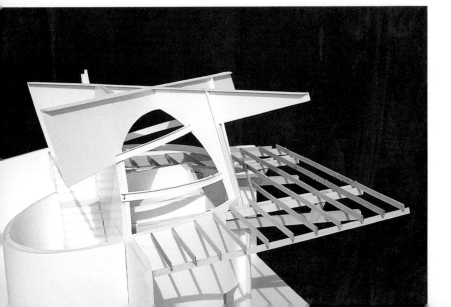

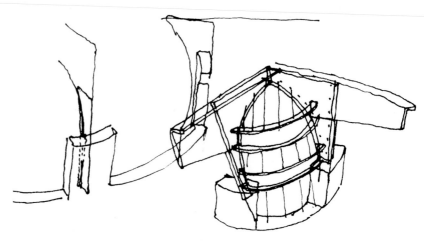

The stair is an event in space. It's a question of how to describe it. There's a deformation of the box that has to do with the movement of the box in space. The stair is pushed into it, which both adds and subtracts. The Box doesn't absorb the stair, and the stair isn't parasitic. The stair could be parasitic if you conceived the Box first and the access second; but it could also be the reverse.

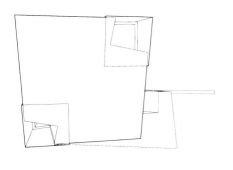

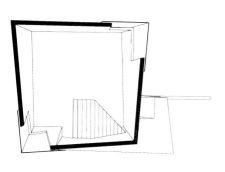

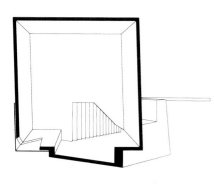

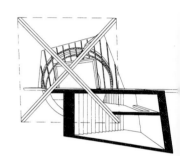

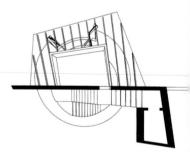

There are windows in the box in opposite corners. The windows are themselves boxes. Each window is an analogous cube.

The anomaly is the floor. The floor is never the box. The order of one is never the order of the other. The floor consists of an expensive white wool carpet that gradually gets dirty: white that becomes black, like the rest.

Very little of the old detail hedonism here—a little in the railing, a little in the skylight, but for the most part it's the object. You confront the object, the object confronts you.

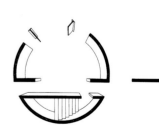

CULVER CITY CA

The Beehive encounters the Box and counters the Box. The Beehive acknowledges the opposition by dancing away to the east.

The Beehive is supported on legs that bend, fold, and incline to redirect the position of the building horizontally as it grows vertically. Steel pipe beams curve horizontally, span the legs. The form of the curve is always established as a consequence of the position of the legs. Every four vertical feet is a new horizontal sequence of beams. At each vertical interval the form of the curve in plan varies as the repositioning legs fold and lean. Spanning the four vertical feet, a sometimes transparent, sometimes translucent skin is fastened to the beams, enclosing the Beehive. Leg bends, curving beam conforms to bending leg, skin conforms to curved steel. That's how the object is made.

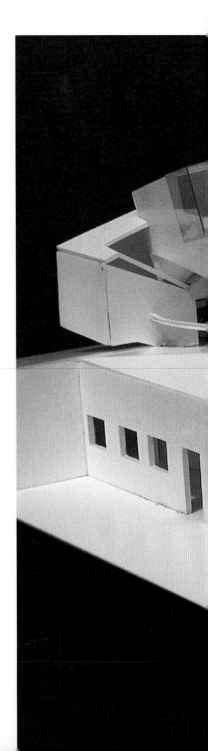

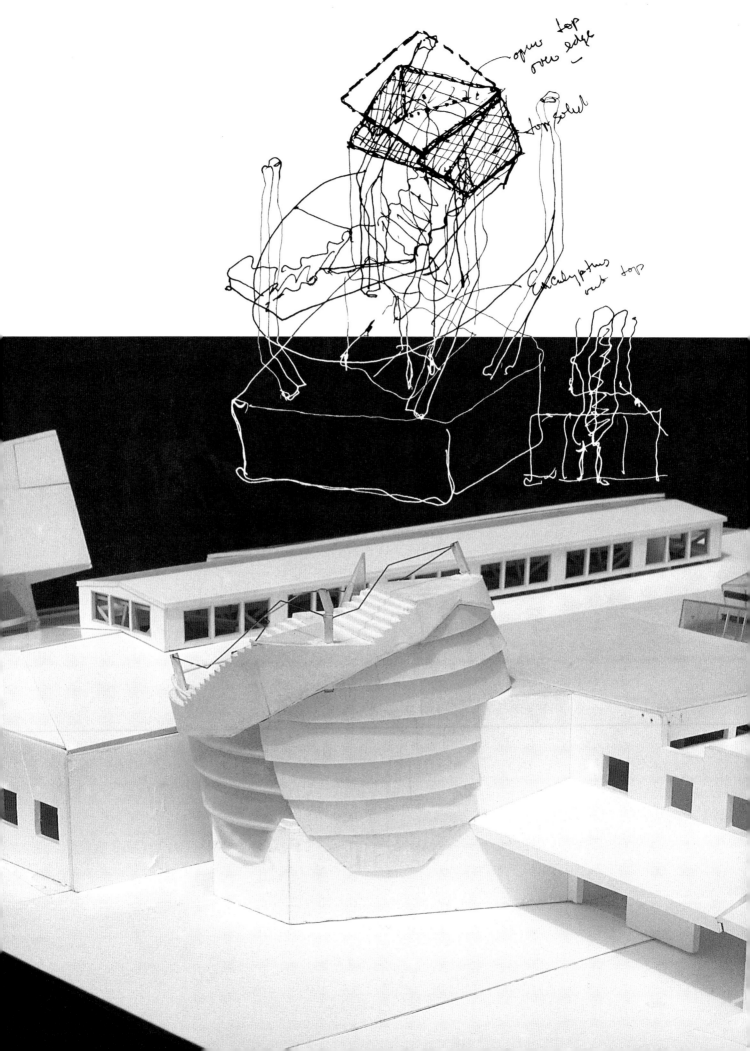

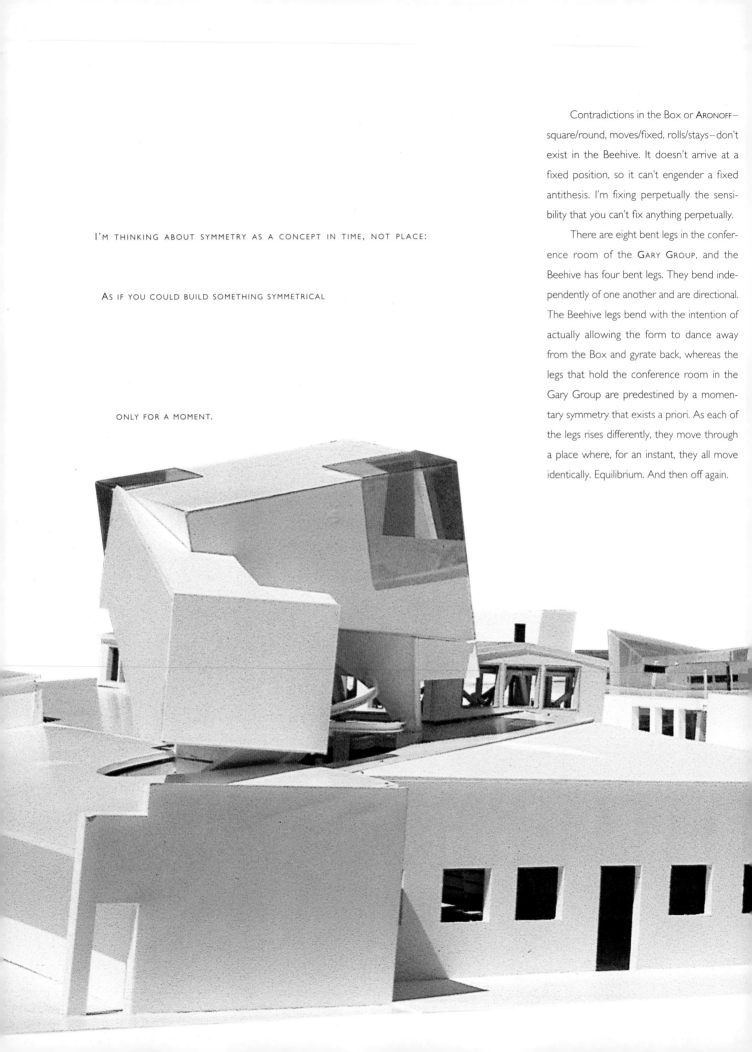

I'M THINKING ABOUT SYMMETRY AS A CONCEPT IN TIME, NOT PLACE:

AS IF YOU COULD BUILD SOMETHING SYMMETRICAL

ONLY FOR A MOMENT.

Contradictions in the Box or ARONOFF— square/round, moves/fixed, rolls/stays—don't exist in the Beehive. It doesn't arrive at a fixed position, so it can't engender a fixed antithesis. I'm fixing perpetually the sensibility that you can't fix anything perpetually.

There are eight bent legs in the conference room of the GARY GROUP, and the Beehive has four bent legs. They bend independently of one another and are directional. The Beehive legs bend with the intention of actually allowing the form to dance away from the Box and gyrate back, whereas the legs that hold the conference room in the Gary Group are predestined by a momentary symmetry that exists a priori. As each of the legs rises differently, they move through a place where, for an instant, they all move identically. Equilibrium. And then off again.

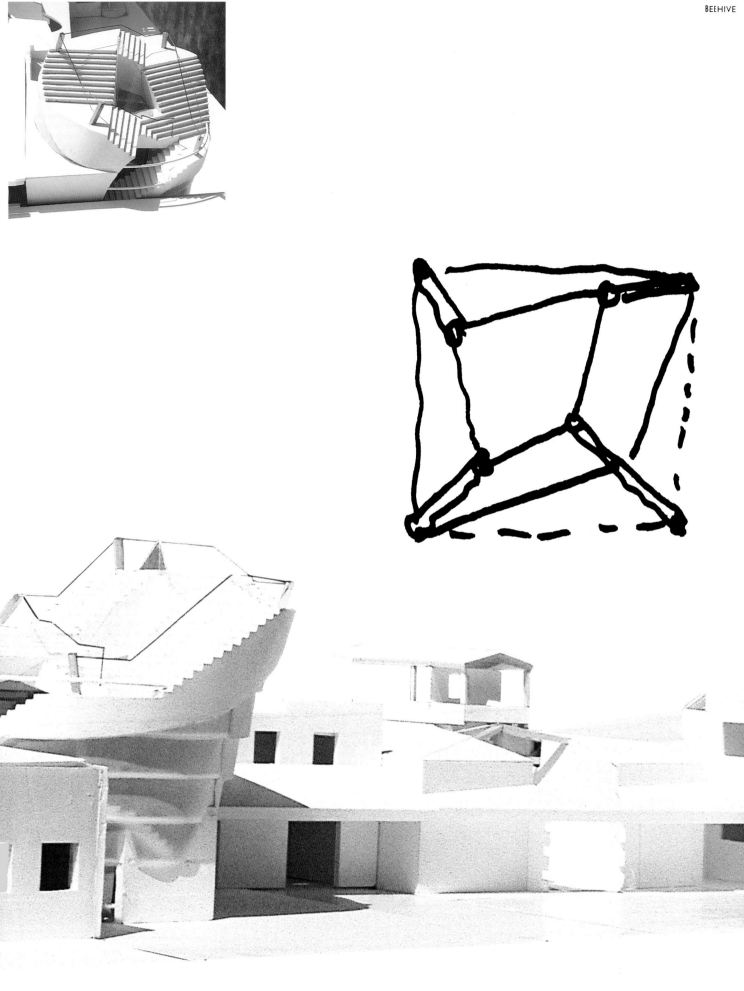

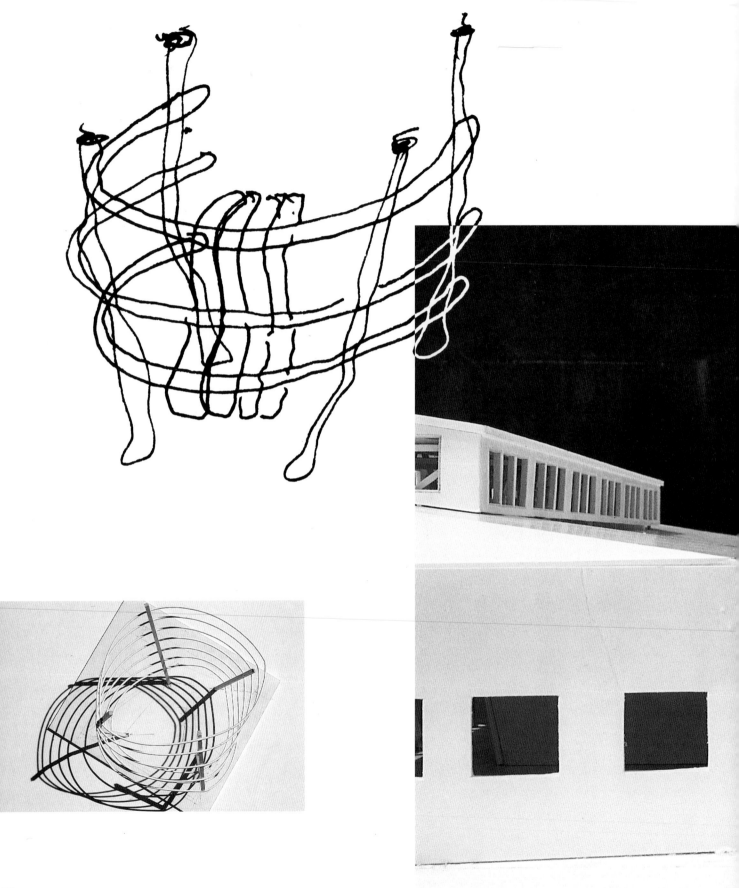

IRS leased a warehouse on the corner of Hayden Street and National Boulevard. Their first concern was positioning the company insignia, which looks like a G-man, a J. Edgar Hoover-type. The name IRS has a not-so-sly, subversive, Hollywood bad-boys connotation. Not establishment, but not too dangerous. The partners requested that the IRS man be placed on the front of the building. Instead, I bent the man into a steel-framed lid at the entrance.

A railroad spur used to off-load at what is now the entry corner. A modular sequence of steel frames carried machines that were moved along an assembly line, then lifted onto trains. These steel frames came from two directions—an L in plan—and met at the corner. I exposed a quasi-pyramid of existing steel to the street by opening up the old wall; the IRS man was folded against the inside of the pyramid. When you're on the street the IRS character looms above your skull.

This L-shaped piece, the designated lobby, is open from floor to roof. A new stairway climbs through the modified melange of old steel on the corner and the man is attached above. A clear acrylic lid covers the steel and the man. The front wall, originally solid, is cut by a big window. You see the new stair and at the top the glazed, steel pyramid open to the sky. There wasn't a smooth, continuous surface to which to attach the acrylic, so I added a number of steel appendages that lift the acrylic away from the frame. The frame and glass have a relationship. It's not just a form over a form, with the two completely unrelated. There's a correlation and a disjunction. Then the man is folded in.

The man is bent against the steel frame to obviate his Madison Avenue identity. The stair contributes because it's another piece that complicates the view of the man. You have to look through a number of things to understand, but you can find him.

IT'S LIKE ONE OF THOSE KID'S GAMES

WHERE YOU'RE LOOKING IN THE JUNGLE
TO FIND THE JAGUAR.

AND IF YOU LOOK AWAY AND LOOK BACK

THE JAGUAR IS GONE.

Overlapping pieces of acrylic cover the man and the discordant pieces of steel. It goes back to a strategy of using steel panels in the TOKYO OPERA HOUSE: the seduction of detail. The joints are quiet. Lines, not mullions.

IRS is a dextrous digression with the man and the glass. Clever in an IQ way. But the disconnected connection between the acrylic and the steel is the real issue: to put a cover on something that can't be covered. Forget the Madison Avenue aspect.

You can stay on the ground level and go down the hall. Or at the entrance you can take the stair to the second floor, but the stair keeps going. After you've passed the second floor you can head up to "nowhere." Nowhere is outside—as soon as you open the door you're on the exterior stair. You go up the stair and reach the top of the building and keep going up.

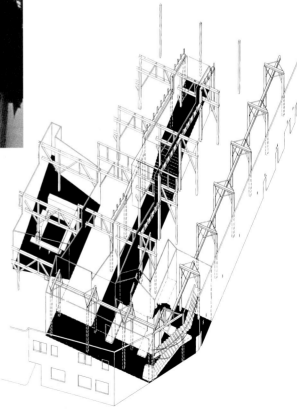

In the rest of the building there is an existing steel frame, a new steel frame, an old wood frame, and trusses. I started putting the program-driven floor planes and partitions into the shed and immediately created anomalies. New floors and walls confront the old wood frame or old steel frame, or the new steel frame, or the old trusses—contests for position and use occur instantly.

There is no remaking. I put the pieces together—old structure, new structure—and program initiated the conflicts, and left them as they were.

SOMETIMES THE JOB IS TO DEFEND THE NEW FROM THE OLD;

SOMETIMES TO PUT THE OLD TOGETHER WITH THE NEW.

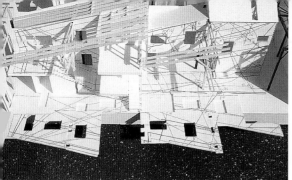

A rectangular courtyard sliced out of the sawtooth shed separates departments and seems to be a place that allows people to bump into each other accidentally. The intent was to avoid organizational simple-mindedness.

I proposed a sun clock sculpture for the walls and floor of the courtyard, a simplified version of what was later developed in the VLA project. But the tenant preferred to use his watch.

Hayden Tower reuses an existing box frame sixty feet high, thirty feet on a side. The steel frame held a big industrial press, but the industry's gone and so is the press. The frame is a permanent scaffold that carries a new series of shapes and spaces.

The triangular property adjoins the SPARCITY right-of-way. At grade is a one-story warehouse; on the roof, parking. Drive in off Hayden Street, up the ramp, onto the roof. Pieces of the lot where cars don't fit become holes in the roof. The holes open to the ground floor— happenstance light courts.

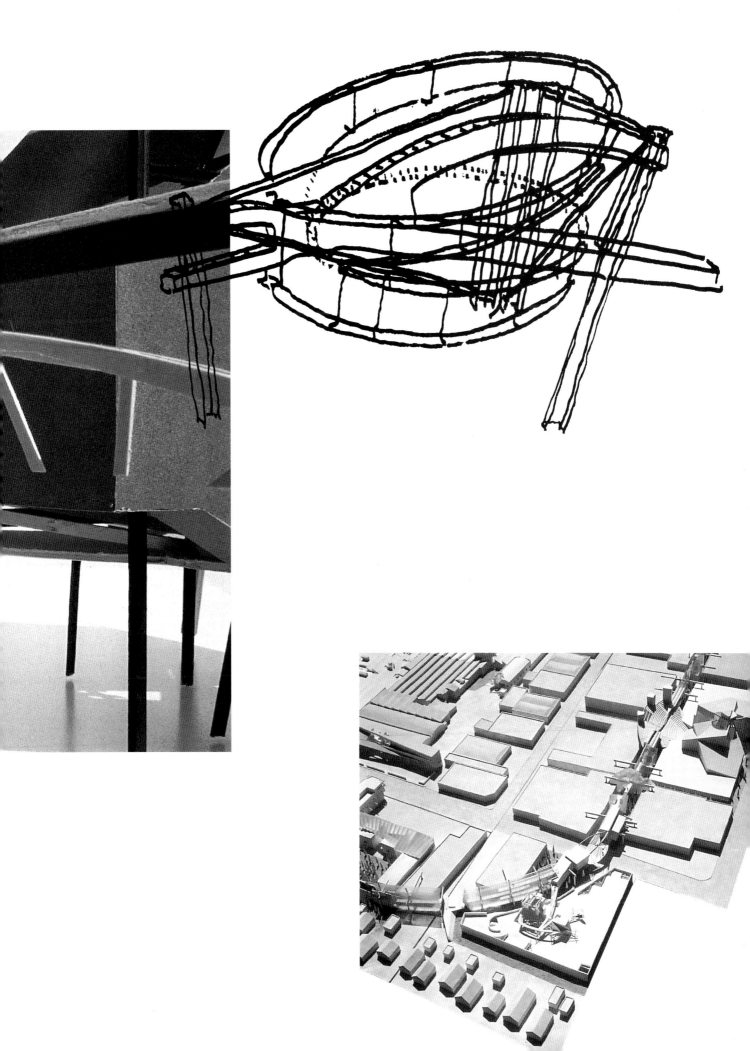

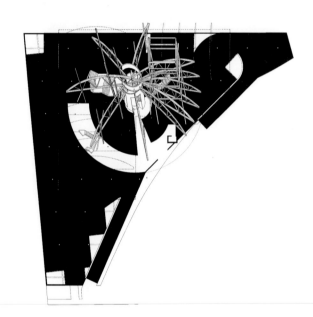

The tower has four wide-flange steel legs. The other old buildings on the site will be torn down. The trusses from the demolished roofs will be salvaged and arranged radially around a steel ring. The ring is a stair-filled funnel cut in the parking deck. The trusses radiate from the ring and extend through the steel frame, supporting a recycled building skin that amends the form of the frame. On level three the old trusses support bridges that connect offices and conference space. Sometimes the tower remains a steel skeleton; in other instances it reforms, following truss profiles. The conference room shape is the precedent for another project across the street. Rotated ninety degrees and stretched three hundred feet, it became the STEALTH.

The fourth level of the tower holds equipment. The original steel frame is revealed here. The tower volume gets smaller at the top and larger at the bottom while the frame stays constant. As the tower grows vertically, it becomes more transparent.

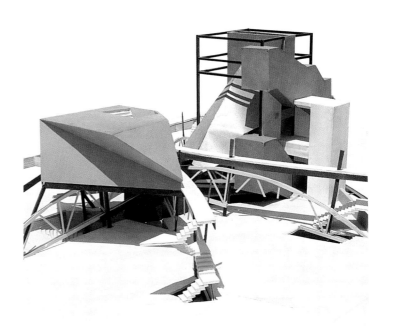

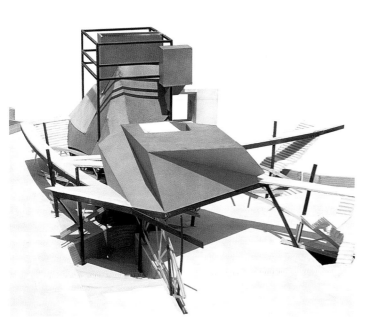

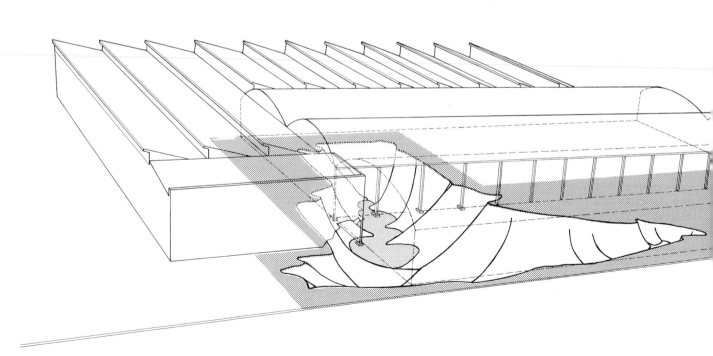

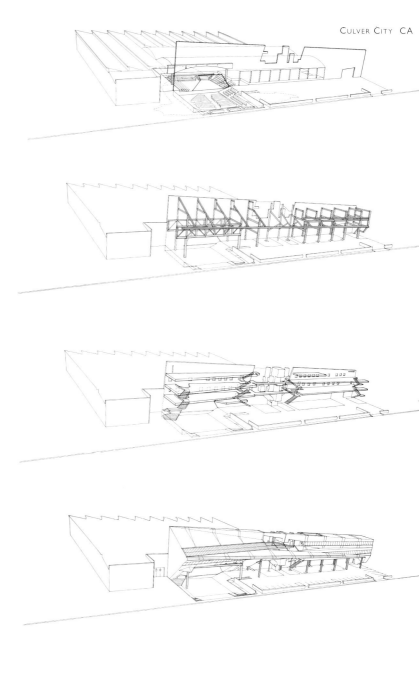

Stealth was precipitated by an excavation to remove petrochemical waste. A lawn is planted in the regraded excavation. Inside the old warehouse structure, a new stage faces the garden, which can hold six hundred seats. There's also an option to combine seating in the old shed with seating in the garden to form a theater-in-the-round.

The conference room at HAYDEN TOWER is the antecedent for Stealth's shape. The floor of the conference room is three-sided; the roof, four-sided. That's the Stealth, rotated ninety degrees.

When the two ends of an object are not synonymous (three-sided and four-sided), how are they connected in a volume with no warps? We experimented, trying to find the answer, a transition between parallel planes, one four-sided, one three-sided.

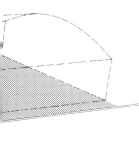

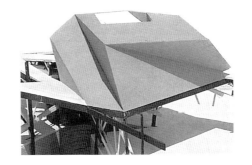

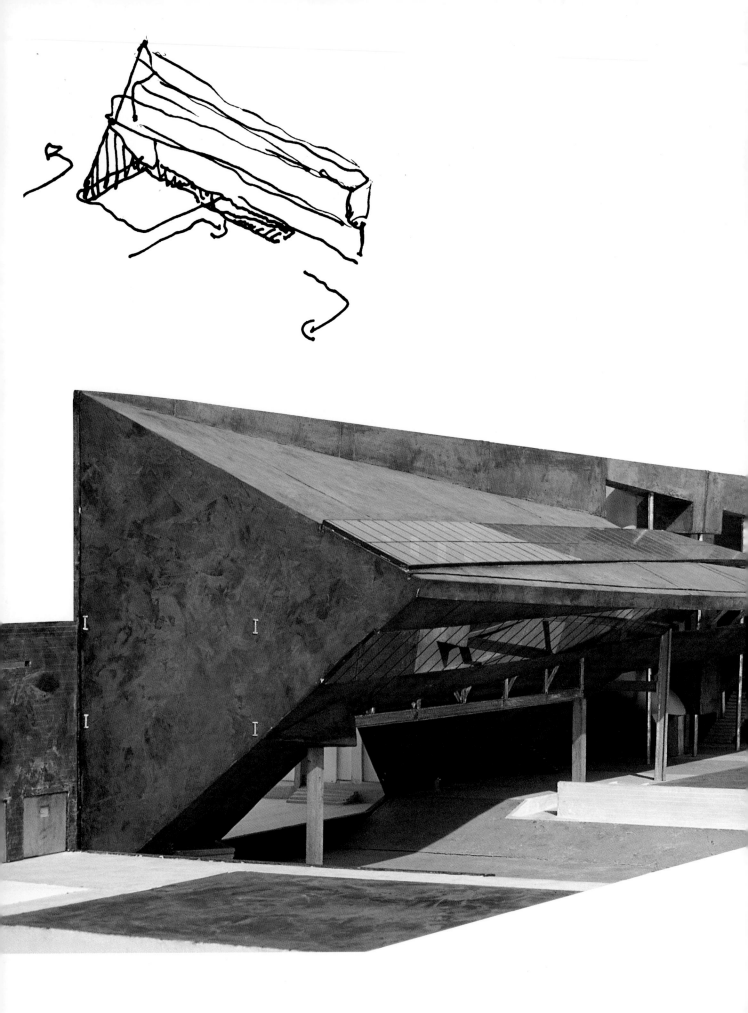

The design remodels Heraclitus: Never step into the same form twice. The north end of the 325-foot-long building is three-sided. The south end, four-sided. The ends are simple, geometric, recognizable. Between the ends, using flat planes, the building section varies constantly over its length. Three becomes four. Four becomes three. The ends are known; in-between, unknown. The movement between the ends is a means to connect them—but expression of movement is also an end. Fixed transition.

Organizational lines derive from the surface planes, wrapping the building section. These lines define the apertures and joints, so a secondary logic, sitting on the alogical building form, is invented.

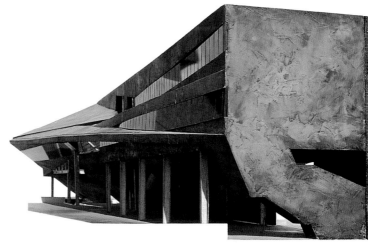

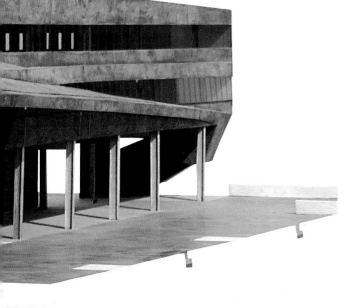

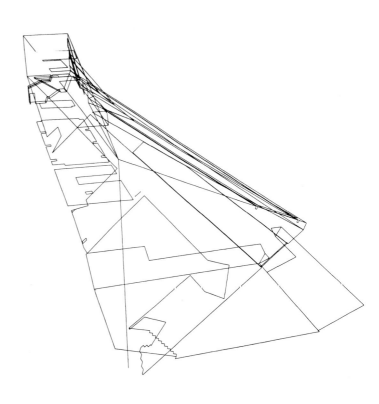

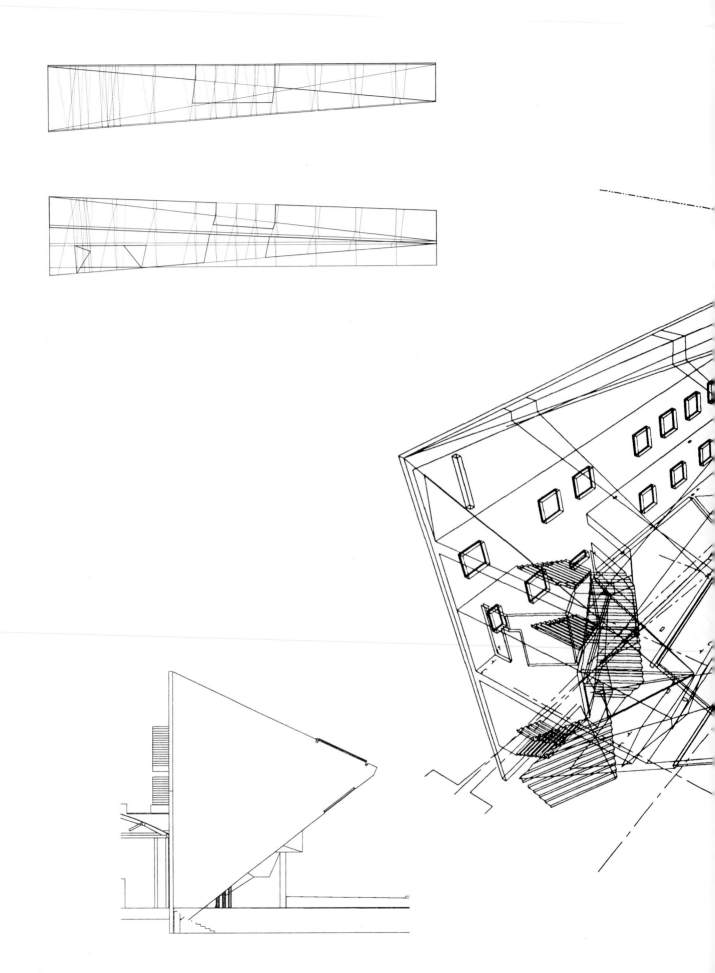

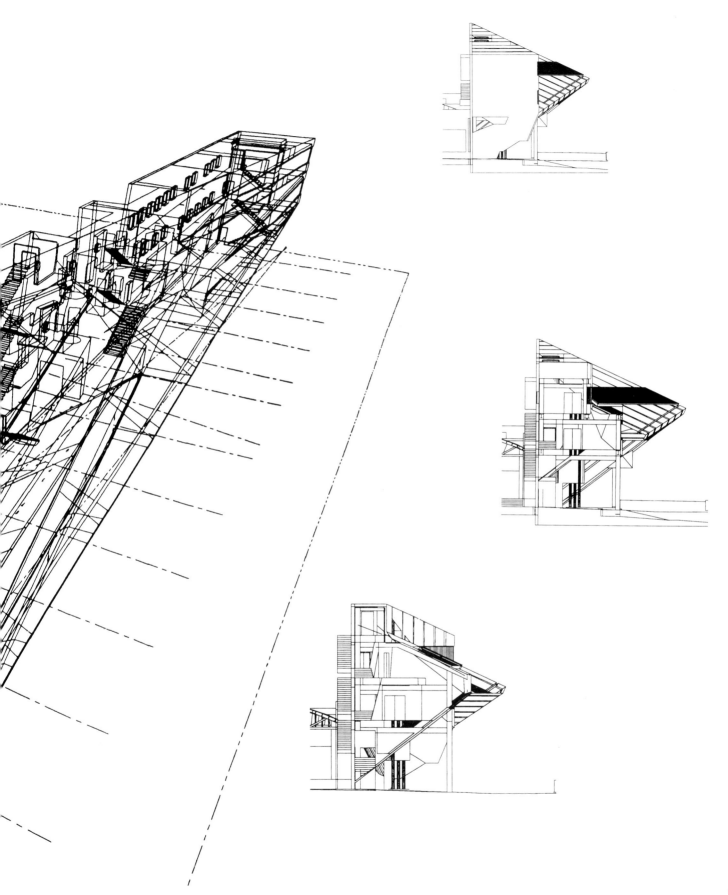

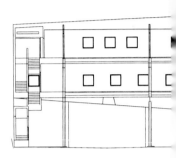

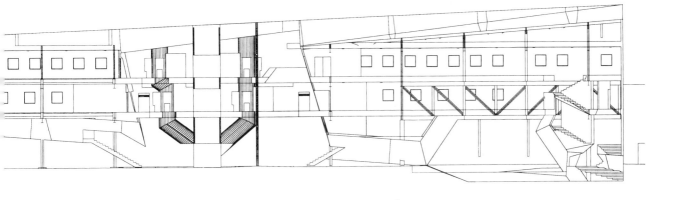

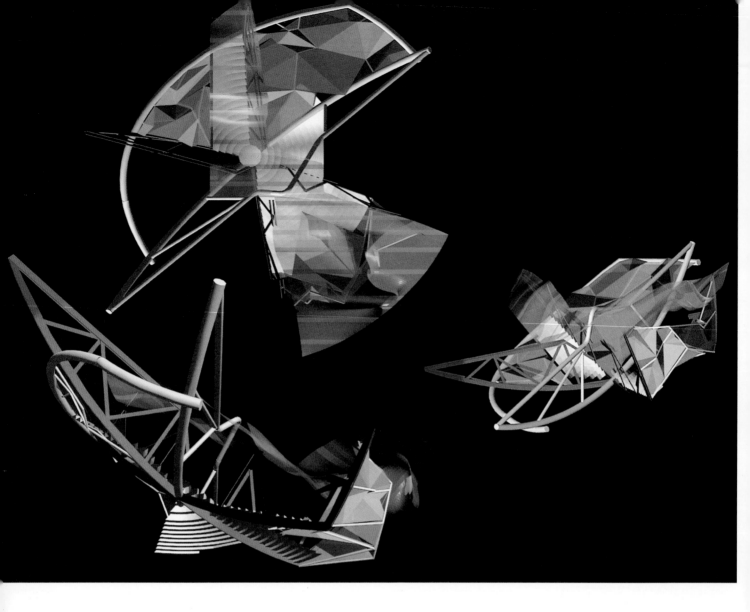

The Green Umbrella represents as architecture what new music represents as sound.

The Los Angeles Philharmonic's experimental music series—The Green Umbrella Concerts—has been produced for eight years at a variety of sites. The concerts will now move to Culver City.

The project has three essential pieces: one is the "umbrella," which is a symbol in two senses—first, it is a symbol of music as experiment, and second, it is a literal sign of the concert series. Why the series was originally called the Green Umbrella no one seems to know. The architecture doesn't question the name; it simply reforms the umbrella physiognomy.

The umbrella form comes from an inverted bowl or dish, like an umbrella without a stem or handle. The analogue umbrella is set at the corner of the building, cutting the roof and hanging over the edge. So the bowl is turned upside down and pushed into the roof.

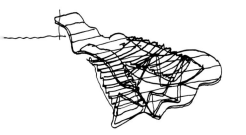

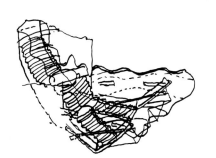

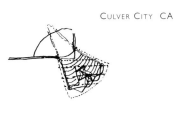

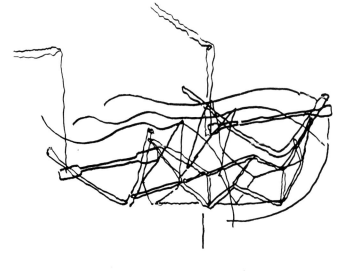

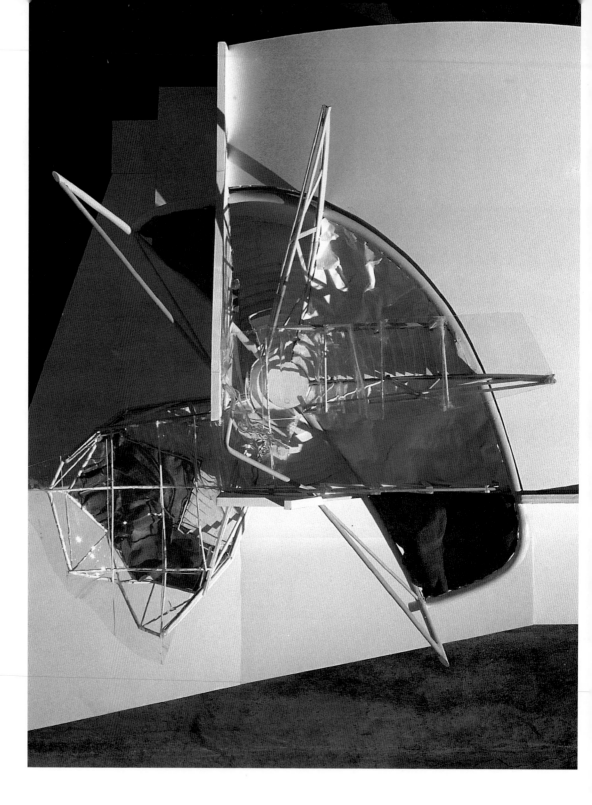

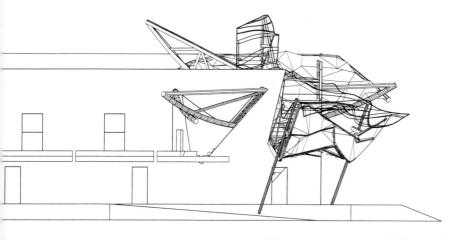

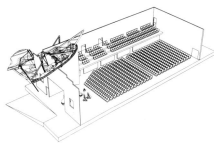

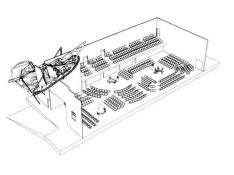

The umbrella holds a bleacher/stair/seating system that supports performers but not an audience. The hall (indented umbrella aside) has a regular orthogonal plan and truss-supported roof. There's a foyer, lobby, and backstage, all of which are done in a utilitarian way. The hall itself seats six hundred people. All of the seating is flexible, so a variety of arrangements is possible: seating at either end, stage in the middle, multiple stages with performers moving from one stage to another.

The umbrella structure is an amalgamation of two existing roof trusses that remain in place and two recycled trusses (salvaged during demolition on the adjacent site) turned upside down. There's also a new steel truss and the concentric stepped bleachers with a glass covering. I thought of the glass as a glacial pushing. The glass originated as a segmented curve conforming to the vaulted roof shape, then deformed to cover the bleacher area in the umbrella. The structures of the bowl and vault are adjusted so that there is continuity between the old roof and the new edge of the bowl. And then the concentric-circle bleachers are inserted into the bowl so the stairs run from the top of the umbrella all the way down to the ground.

Concerts can be performed outside, or outside and inside in combination. The umbrella would be used for concerts outside, though there's been discussion of having the performers in the umbrella and the audience both inside and outside, in which case part of the audience could hear but not see the musicians.

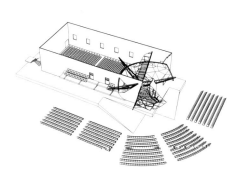

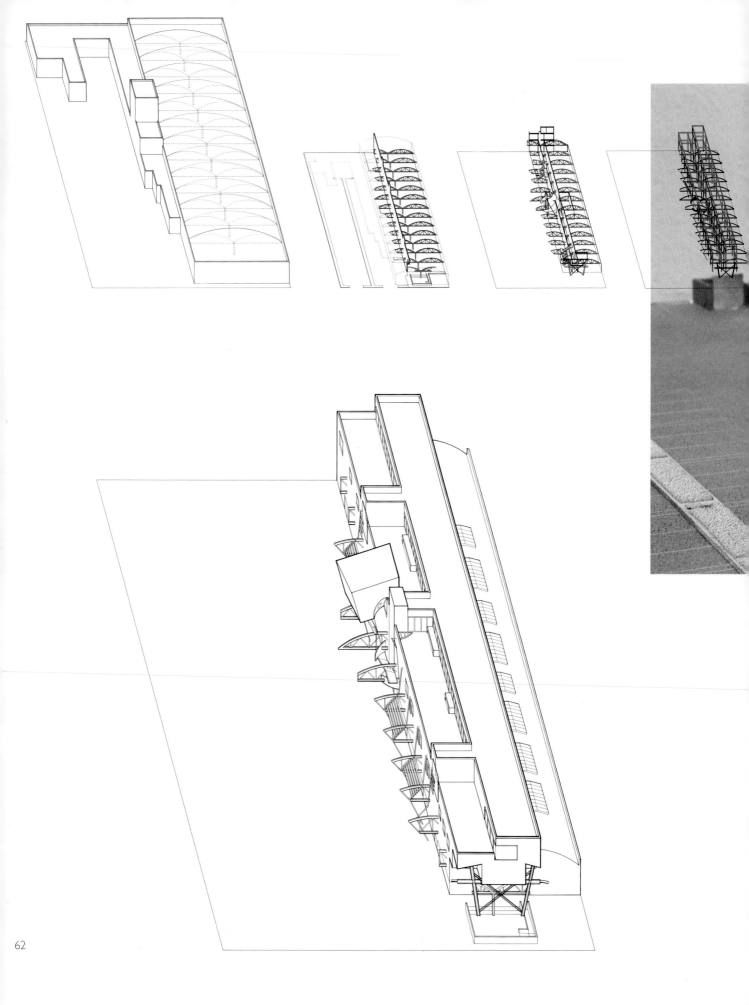

None of the pieces in the series—R1, R2, R3 or PSF—has the external power of SAMITAUR or HAYDEN TOWER. This project is more introverted. The series is as much about evolution as about form, but the evolution is not Darwinian. It's a xerox job: one building is four buildings.

The building was pragmatic at first. Parking lot size determined the first cut. Four existing buildings on the site are demolished, with parts of one, 240 feet long, running east-west from the front to the back of the site, retained. Its roof is carried on parallel pairs of bowstring trusses. The roof is removed, the bowstring trusses and posts remain, everything else is knocked down.

Along the south perimeter of the building a wall is dropped in to accommodate the parking dimension on the site—car, aisle, double car, aisle, car, wall. That starts the envelope.

An orderly steel frame—tube columns and wide-flange beams—is deposited over the trusses. The method is orthogonal. That frame carries three office floors. The center column of the typical bowstring pair lands in the double-loaded corridor that runs down the center of the building.

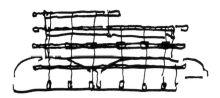

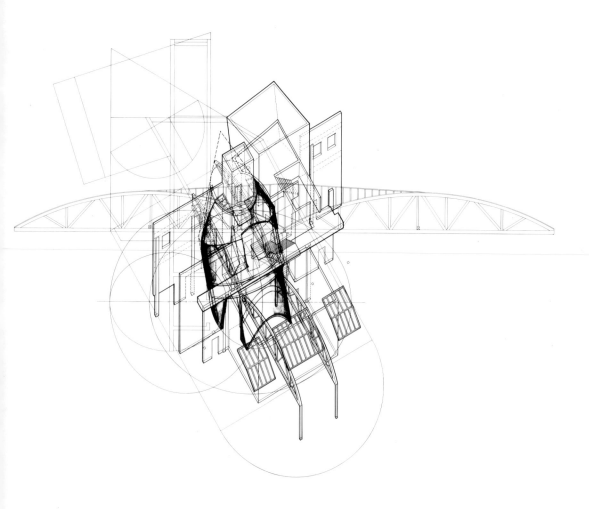

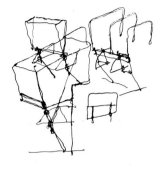

The lobby is an anomaly within the orthogonal order of the steel frame and wood trusses. Ditto the Hayden Street elevation, the conference room behind the lobby, and the tipped box on the second floor. The lobby is more complicated than, but not unrelated to, LAWSON/WESTEN as a spatial experiment. Both spaces begin with a recognizable category of geometry and end with a super- (but not supra-) geometry.

The lobby is an object/volume leaned into the south wall and cut at the exterior building face. The shape presses against the front wall and is fossilized, leaving its imprint as a glass aperture. There are bridges from each floor to the black-block elevator core. The lobby extends inside to outside, crosses the exterior wall, and cuts the tipped conference block. The lobby is exposed, in section, on the front of the building so the elevation is a section. Inside you get the volume. In the adjacent rooms on the three office floors you get the outside of the inside. But you never get the shape as an entity.

The second permutation is a house, R2, produced for an exhibit. R2 confirms the IBIZA PASEO principle: The meaning of a building always precedes or supersedes its current use and is more durable than its current utility.

What characteristics justify the label "house"? That didn't interest me. The museum tried to figure out what made it a house, but that was their concern.

R2 is the exception to the R system, the interruption in the frame. The anomaly is assigned a label: house. Ancillary pieces that abet the function of the office building are gone.

The frame is removed. The trusses remain and the free truss ends are supported on pipes. R2 is a different color and was named Peanut Butter House—something homey—so nobody would be terrorized.

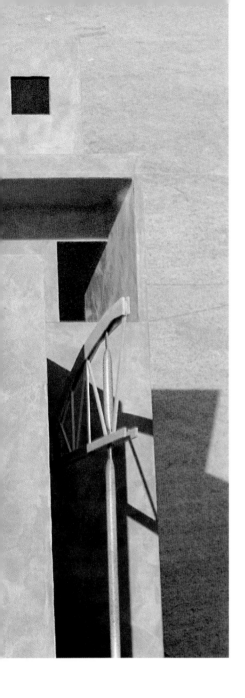

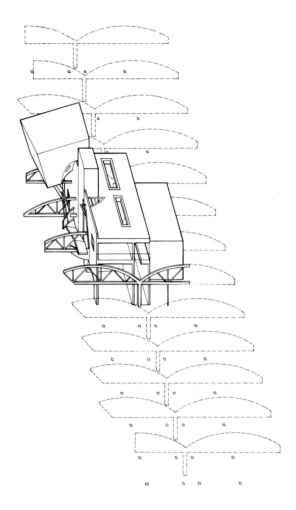

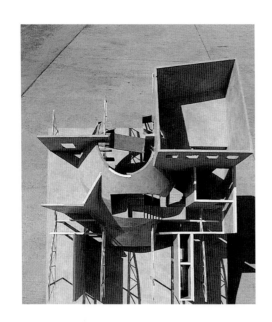

THE ODD EVENT IN EVEN

CIRCUMSTANCES IS NO LONGER ODD

BECAUSE THERE'S NO EVEN HERE.

The perimeter is glazed. The volumes are now understandable from the outside, through the glass. It is no longer just an introverted space. The relationship between the outside of the building and the outside of the lobby is available to the adjoining spaces and to the exterior. The anomaly is no longer an anomaly because the lobby was an exception to a very consistent, long office block that is now removed. The fourth floor was pulled off, and its east edge is the end of the conference room. In R1 the office block was a foil for the lobby. Now, no foil. The surrounding orthogonal space is gone, although the surgery is at right angles. Does the surgery imply the prospect of the original block?

R3 is an act of contrition and brings to the public what always was a public space. R1 had the enormous lobby reserved for a private few. Like much of the work that's been done in Culver City, the lobby belonged to the office tenant. The first argument for the theater was that the public would walk through that space. The public space becomes public.

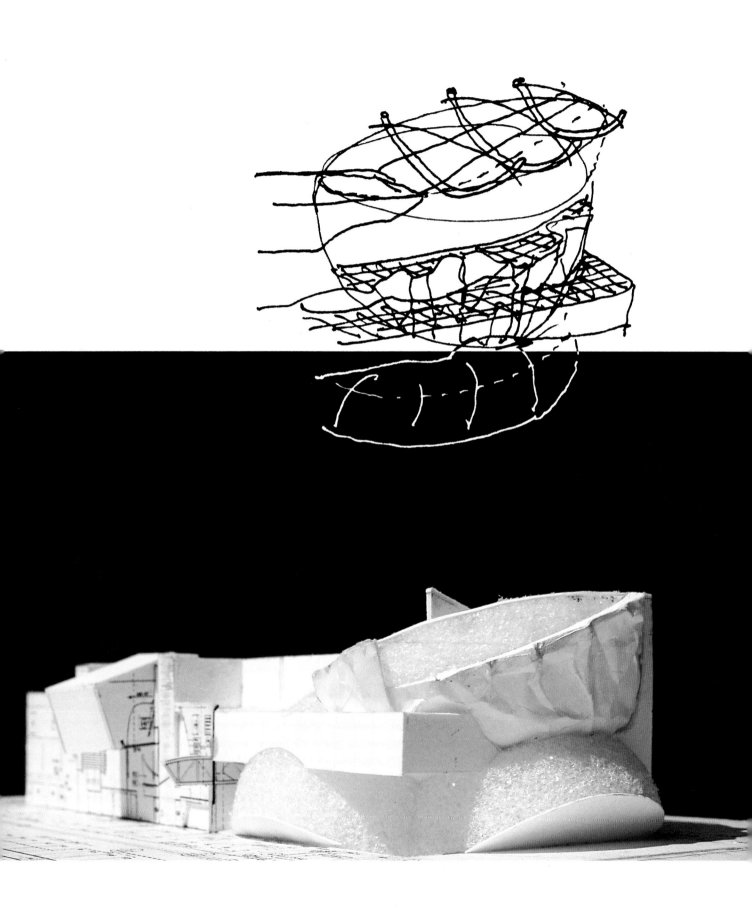

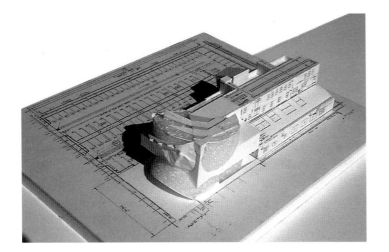

The lobby takes you west to offices and east to the theater. R3 becomes a theater by interacting with the orthogonal order of the circulation system and the box itself—the three-sphere strategy and the orthogonal organization of the frames. The two intervene and work off each other. There is an equity. I wouldn't say an anomaly exists anymore because the theater is so strong. An anomaly is an exception to a system that predominates. If anything, the frame becomes the anomaly here. Either there is an equity and no anomaly or the frame has become the anomaly in the theater. Now, how that would actually work itself out in terms of those original trusses is only hypothetical, because the project didn't go that far. It didn't work on the site. The site was not large enough to accommodate it and so the theater had to move, and it moved pretty quickly—to INCE.

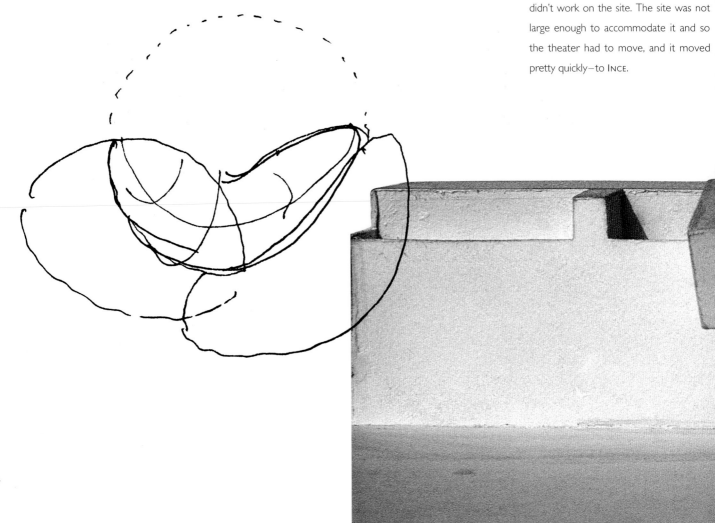

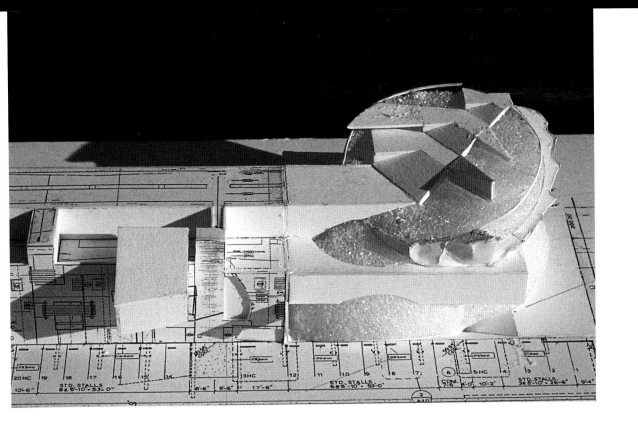

CULVER CITY CA

PSF is the fourth permutation in this series. The program is again an office building with an increase in square footage from thirty thousand to fifty thousand. The trusses, the frames, the lobby, the walls all remain—but now there are five boxes on the west side of the building. The boxes were designed to hold both program and mechanical equipment—that's the origin of the grills. The grill elevation is restrained. It doesn't gyrate.

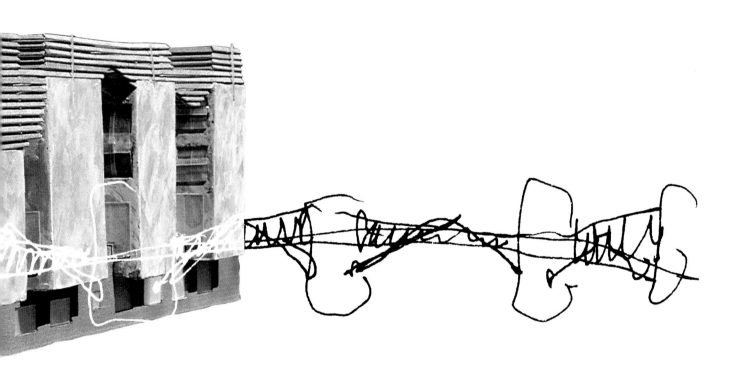

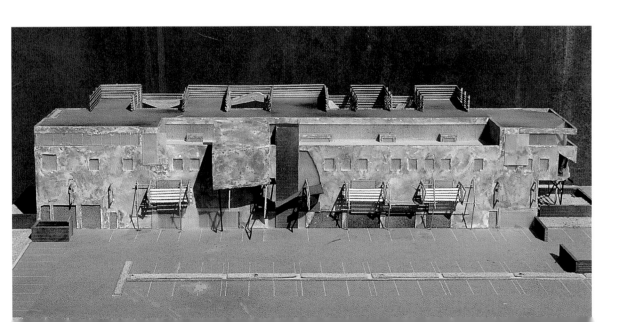

77

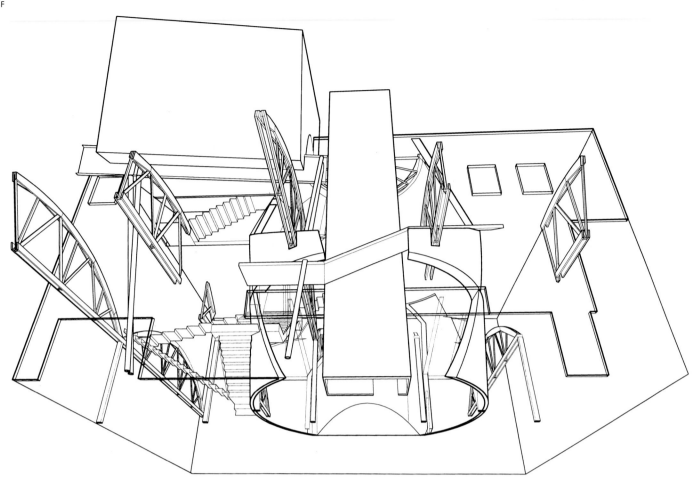

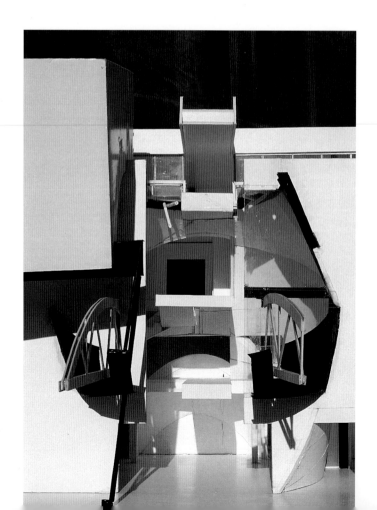

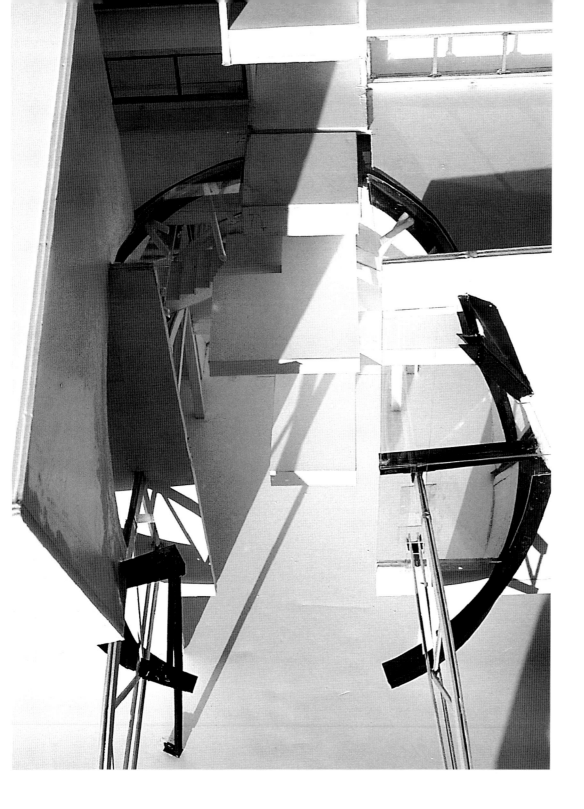

PSF added, externally, the blocks. The blocks are on the north side and initially came riding over the original sawtooth-supported roof. Actually they extend a little beyond the roof and they were done in a pragmatic way in order to increase the square footage. They follow more or less the position of the original R-grid and frame; once you have the grid or frame on level one, two, three, or four, it can be extended vertically and horizontally, which starts to position the walls, so the walls of the blocks then follow the original grid. They are not exceptions to the grid.

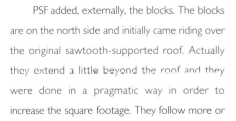

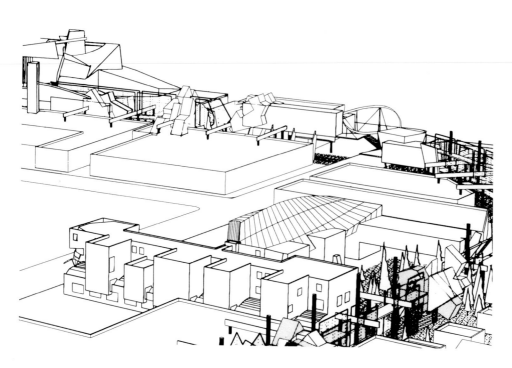

The second phase of PSF originates at the first-phase lobby. It grows off that lobby – still the fundamental organizational piece in the building – and stretches into the next site or piece of property, which the owner has purchased. But it has a very different strategy for making itself. It actually goes from vertically acknowledging the elevator core that splits the lobby to transform into what is essentially a horizontal building. It goes from a vertical to a horizontal building; but it has its own order, its own strategy, and its own ideas.

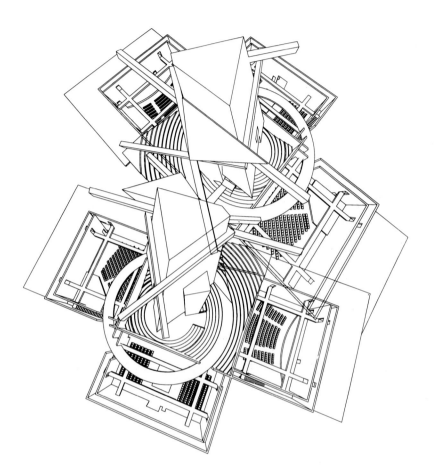

This project abuts the SPARCITY right-of-way. The land is owned by a redevelopment agency that's interested in reinvigorating an industrial zone with no industry. So the city's prepared to go in and build a parking lot. Build the parking structure and in the midst of it, we build an office building. Next, cut a hole, hollow it out of the office building, and fill it with a theater—a big, introverted public space, an amphitheater. There's a structure coming out of the amphitheater called the Tepee. It's residual pieces of the amalgamation of three office blocks and the hole. Stairs and elevators in the Tepee go up six floors. Down the elevator, you're thirty feet below grade at the stage level of the atrium theater.

The Tepee doesn't go down to stage level; it stops to form a canopy for the outdoor stage. At the bottom of the amphitheater you can move laterally into any of three interior theaters that are externally shapeless. The outdoor theater becomes a stairway to the three flexible theaters inside, boxes holding two hundred to three hundred people. Surrounding the theaters on the outside of the inside are public lobbies, and on the inside of the inside, workshops, dressing rooms, and construction areas. The three black boxes are each about thirty feet high with intermediate grids running through them. Theater in the corner, thrust theater, theater-in-the-round: ways of arranging seating and producing dramatic art in forms with no exterior form.

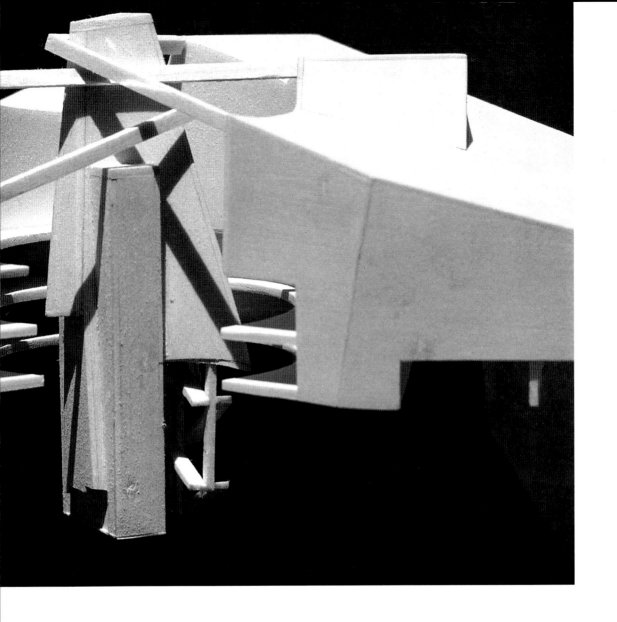

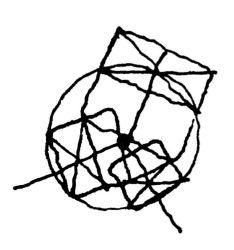

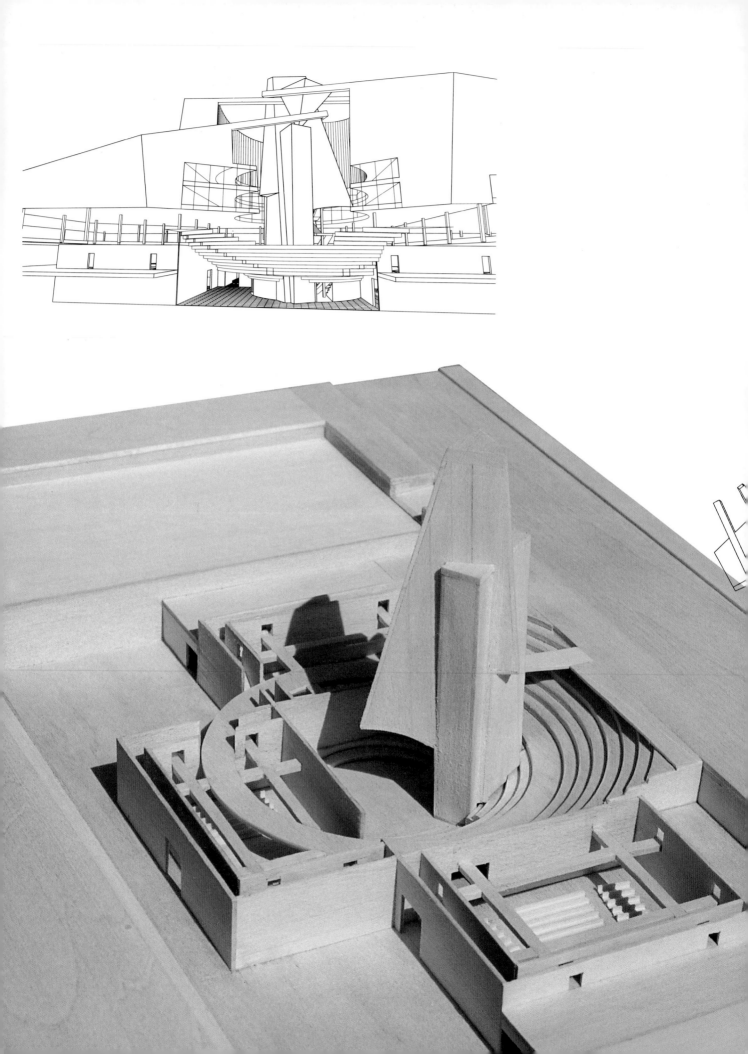

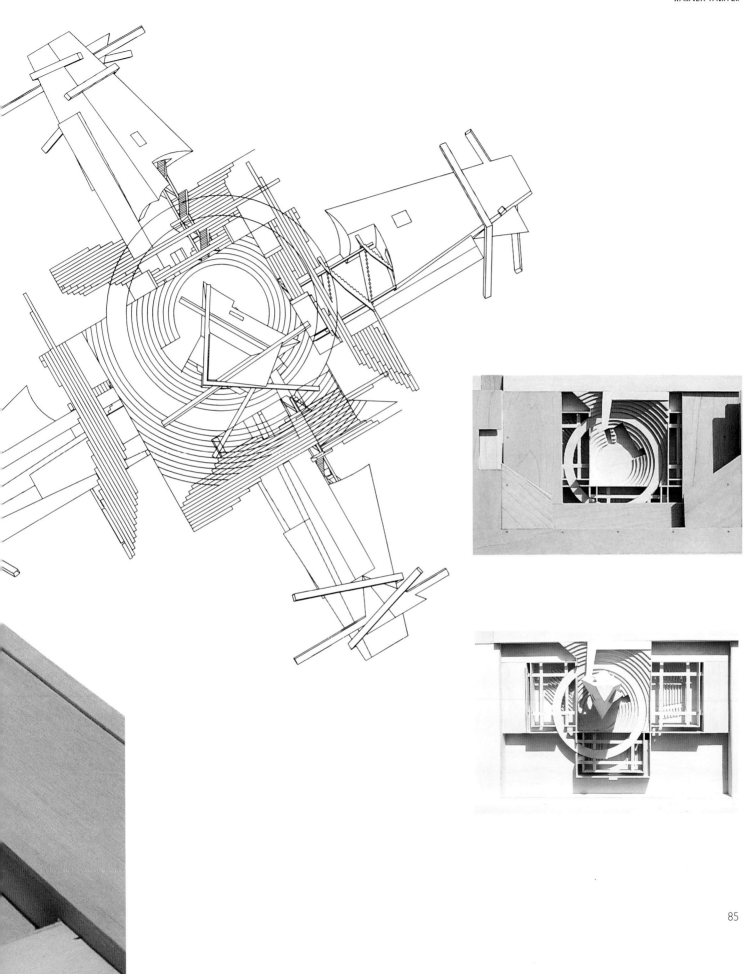

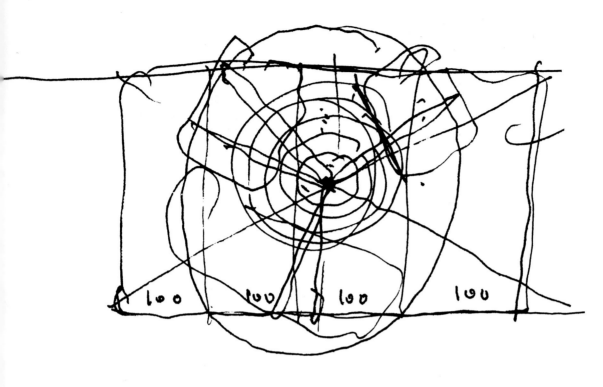

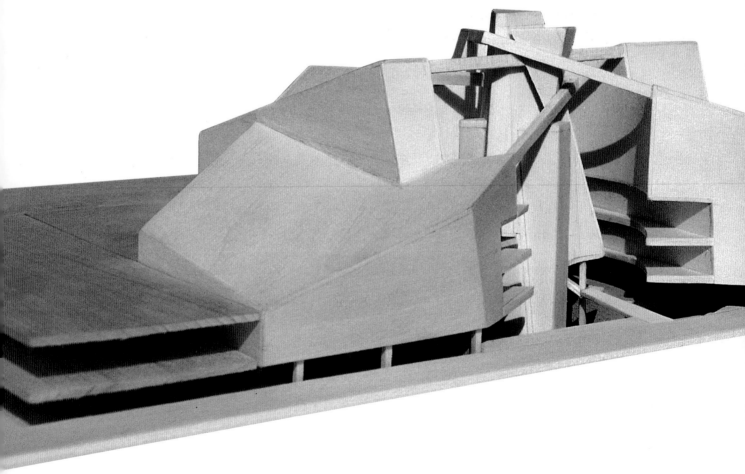

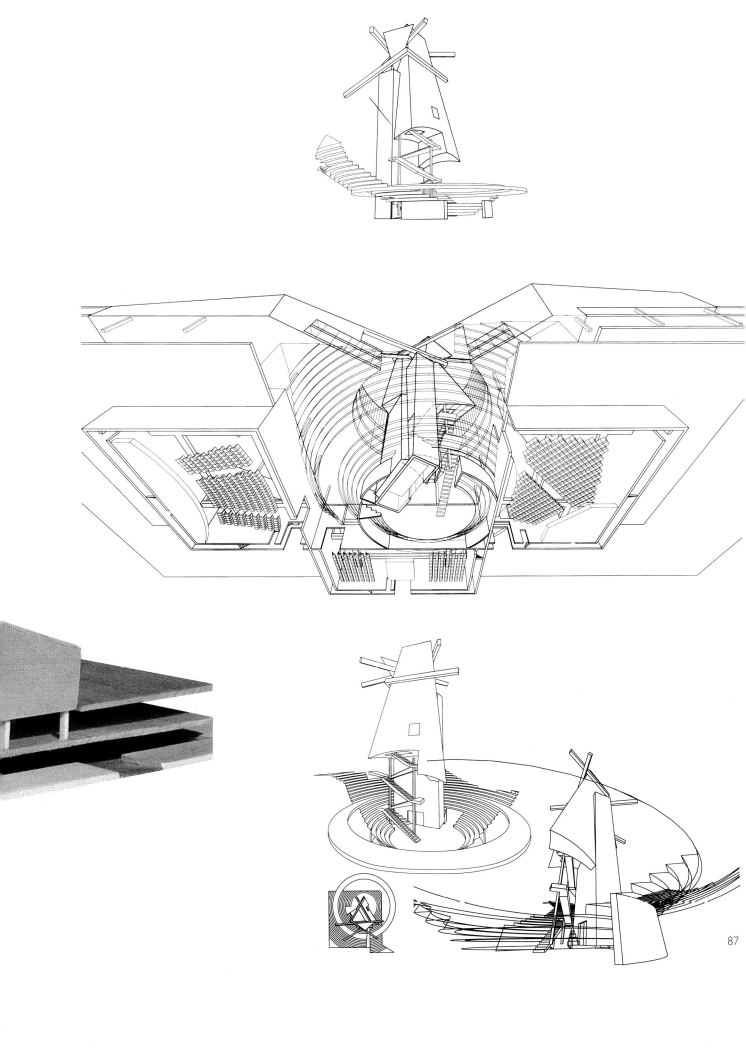

SPARCITY

CULVER CITY/LOS ANGELES CA

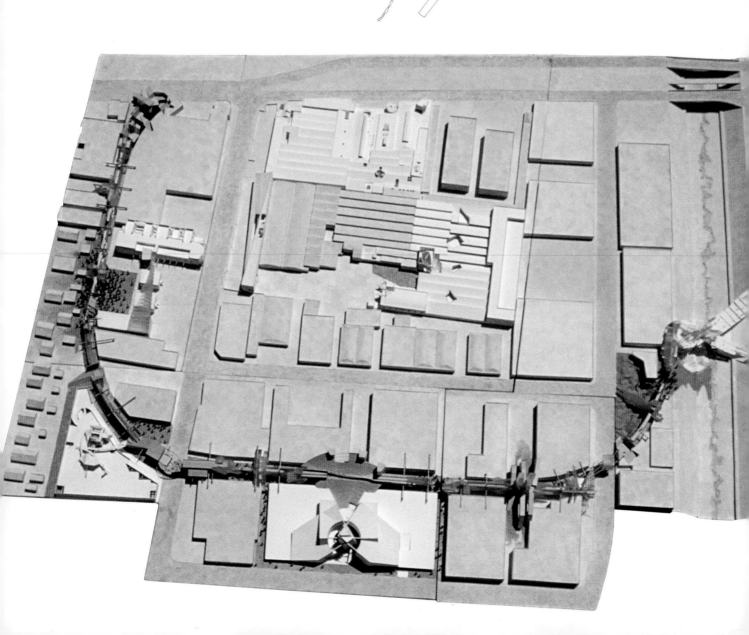

The SPARCITY proposal offers an alternative to property lines and street grids—the prospect of a different sociology.

SPARCITY is in the Hayden Tract. Take over a dormant railway right-of-way, reconstitute it, make it a park, and run a tram through it with buildings above.

SPARCITY is a chameleon. It changes forms: it's park, bridge, office—and nothing if the neighbors yell. It's congenial, cooperative, and produces linkages. It jumps the tracks and binds the community together. It offers to extend or amend what's already there, or to infill what's not—a Salvation Army of city planning.

I argued that the site should be designated an architecturally free zone. Take the area where SPARCITY exists and get rid of all the regulations: no setbacks, no height limits, no car counts, nothing. But that wouldn't mean no standards. Each architect, each developer would have to discuss each project strategically: its aspirations, its consequences. The bureaucracy, the developer, and the architect would begin again with each proposal. No a priori rules.

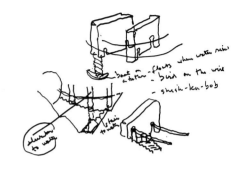

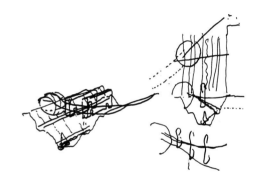

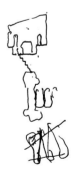

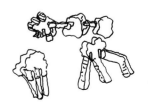

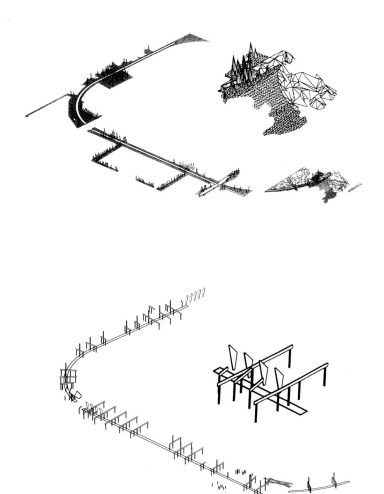

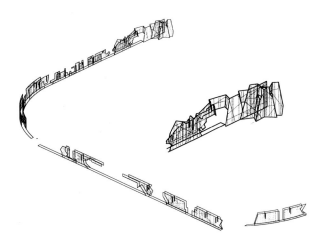

The first step is to design the entire right-of-way as a public park at grade—a continuous pedestrian path from one end to the other. The transformations in the park acknowledge potential changes in use both in and adjacent to the right-of-way.

A structural frame of columns and beams is built. Columns land in the right-of-way or in or on the adjacent buildings. The structure starts or stops, depending on the interrelation of properties adjacent to the SPARCITY site, and will carry a variety of future building types in the air.

A glass-enclosed system of pedestrian walkways above grade, lifted on the new columns and beams, traverses the right-of-way. Like the structural frames, the glass curtain also starts and stops, depending on events in the right-of-way and the associations with adjoining properties.

Anomalies—special purpose buildings—attach to the structural frame, curtain wall, and landscape as various opportunities for unique building types present themselves. The anomalies occur over the pedestrian walks, above existing sheds, on unbuilt properties on either side of the right-of-way, over the landscape, or integrated within it.

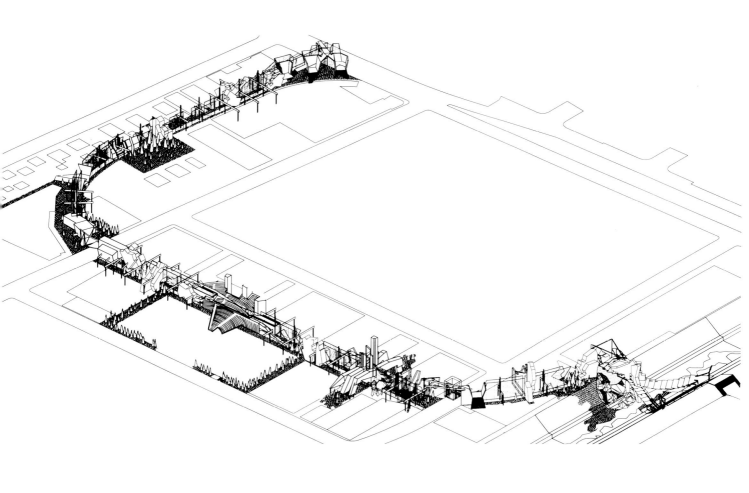
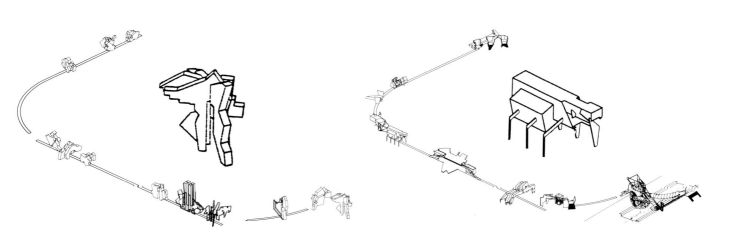

The entire project is, in a sense, a bridge: a bridge over a park for the entire length of the project, and a series of specific bridges over streets that cross the right-of-way and finally over the Los Angeles River. SPARCITY bridges not only represent ways to go from point to point, but are themselves destinations.

What's interesting about my relationship with the developers, the Smiths, is that for a long time we had no planning strategy, just an evolving perception: define what the city could be as we go. The programmatic content of SPARCITY is still hypothetical. SPARCITY looks very definitive aesthetically, and it is, but the definitive aesthetic is rubber. How it would stretch or bend or twist or start or stop would be dependent on any number of future decisions about the property and those adjacent to the right-of-way.

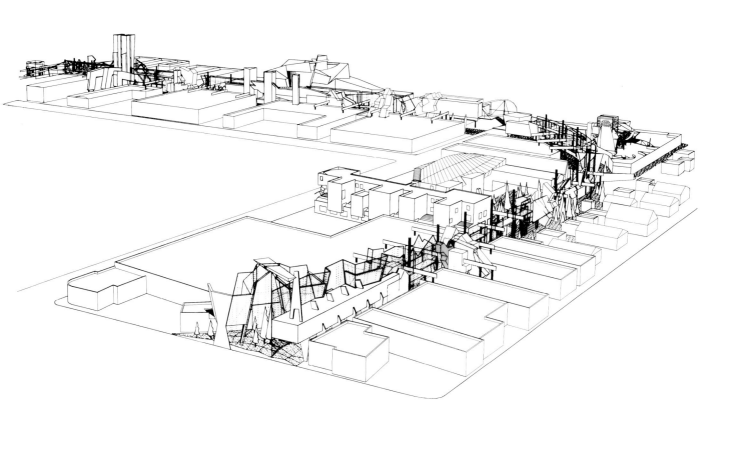

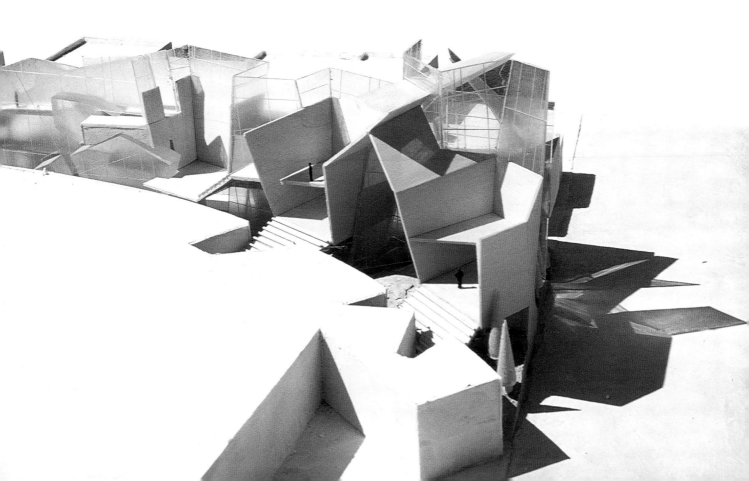

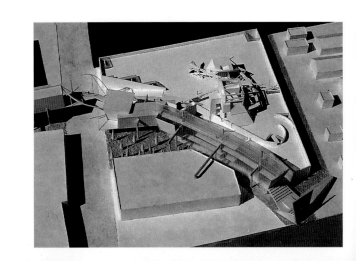

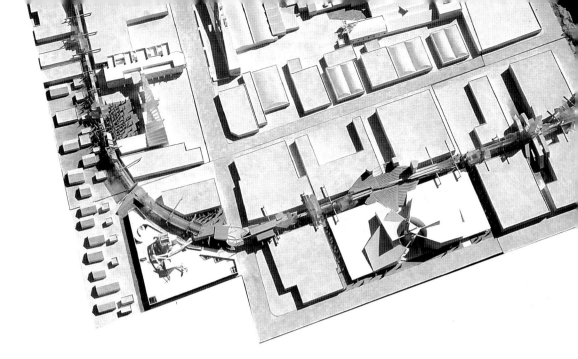

SPARCITY is a sign of a certain optimism. I wouldn't call it naive optimism. It's irrepressible. Architecture keeps coming. Can't stop it. The Smiths are keeping the prospect alive. Frederick's a Republican. He writes checks. What interests him is an issue larger than the architectural object: the prospect of remaking the city and the civility of American cities in the twenty-first century. Whatever the differences between Frederick's approach to making the city (or foreseeing the next city) and mine, we share a fundamental conviction about architecture's responsibility.

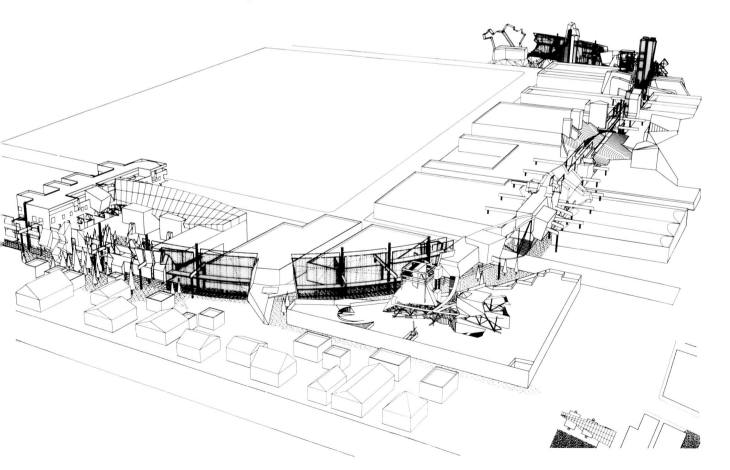

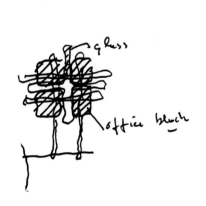

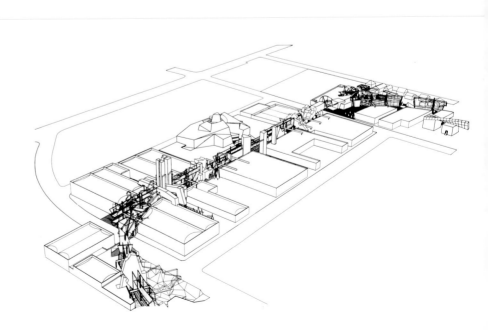

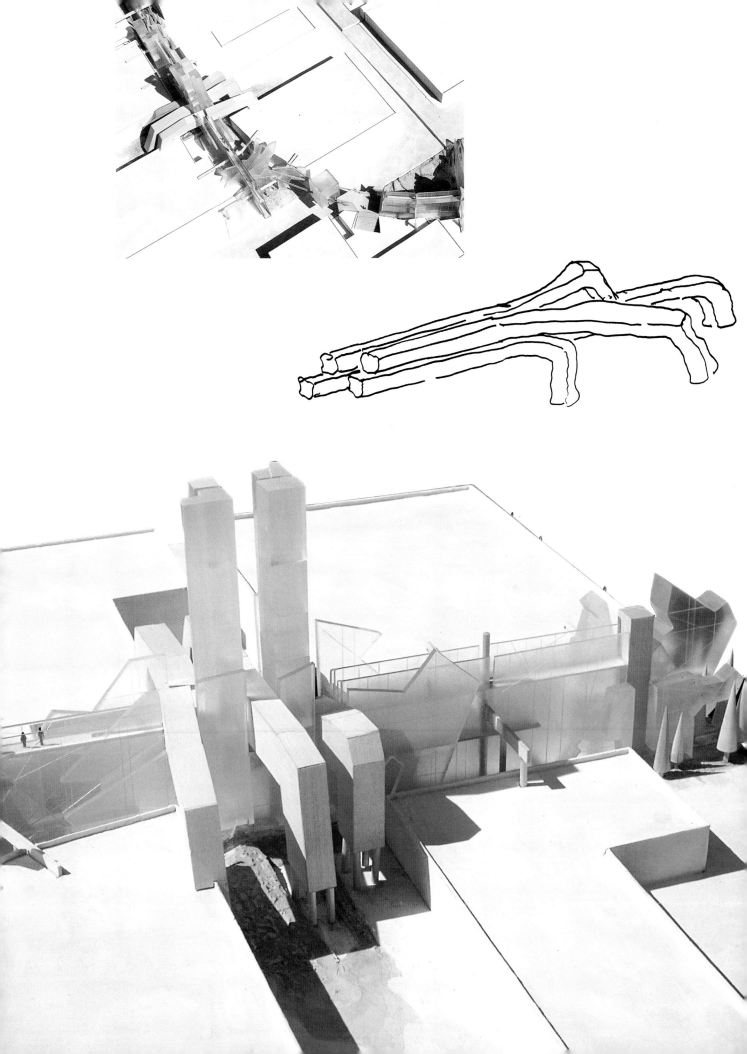

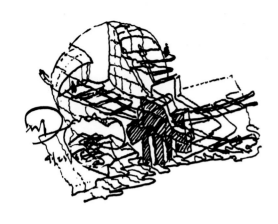

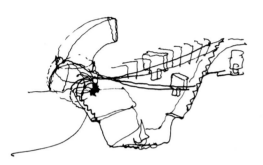

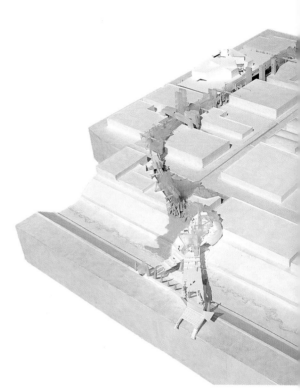

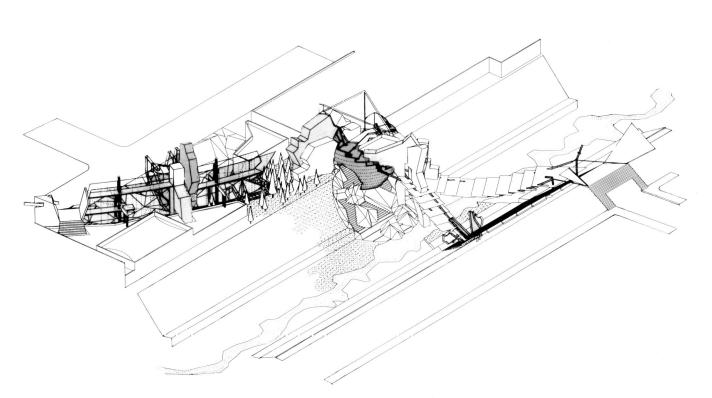

In 1989, Frederick Smith asked me to revise the interior of the sawtooth building that's under the boardroom of what came to be Samitaur.

The conversation wasn't about a building. There was no site, no project, no program—simply a discussion of how we could provide more space for one of Smith's tenants. I proposed that we put a block in the air, the essential gesture, the first gesture of the building. It was an opportunity to use the air rights.

The block is one hundred meters long, in the air over the road, lifted on girders supported by pipes. The amalgamation of beams, girders, and columns is not strange so much as it is an order you haven't seen and couldn't anticipate.

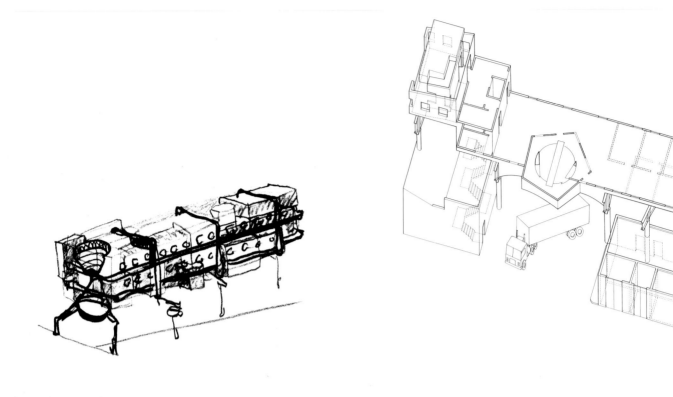

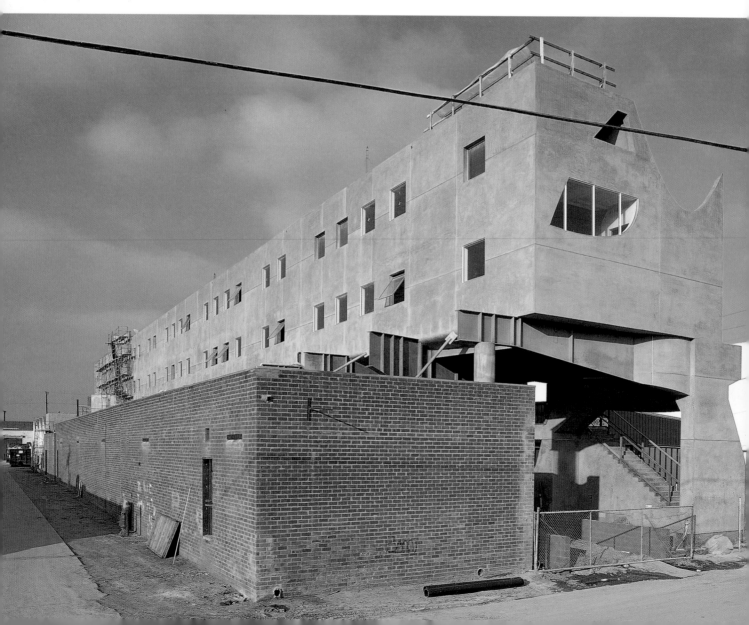

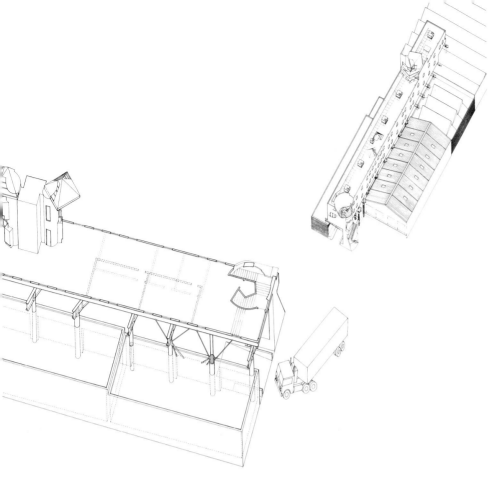

The block is limited in height to forty-eight feet. The width is limited by the fire department—you can't traverse an imaginary line over the existing buildings below. So the building can only be over the road; it can't be over the adjacent buildings—although I abrogated that a little. Underneath the block there's a required clearance of fifteen feet for trucks. So Samitaur is the block, the limits of the block, or cutting out of the block, but never adding to the block. On the underside it's not quite the block—there are pieces cut away so it opens up and lets more light in. The light moves and the structure dances.

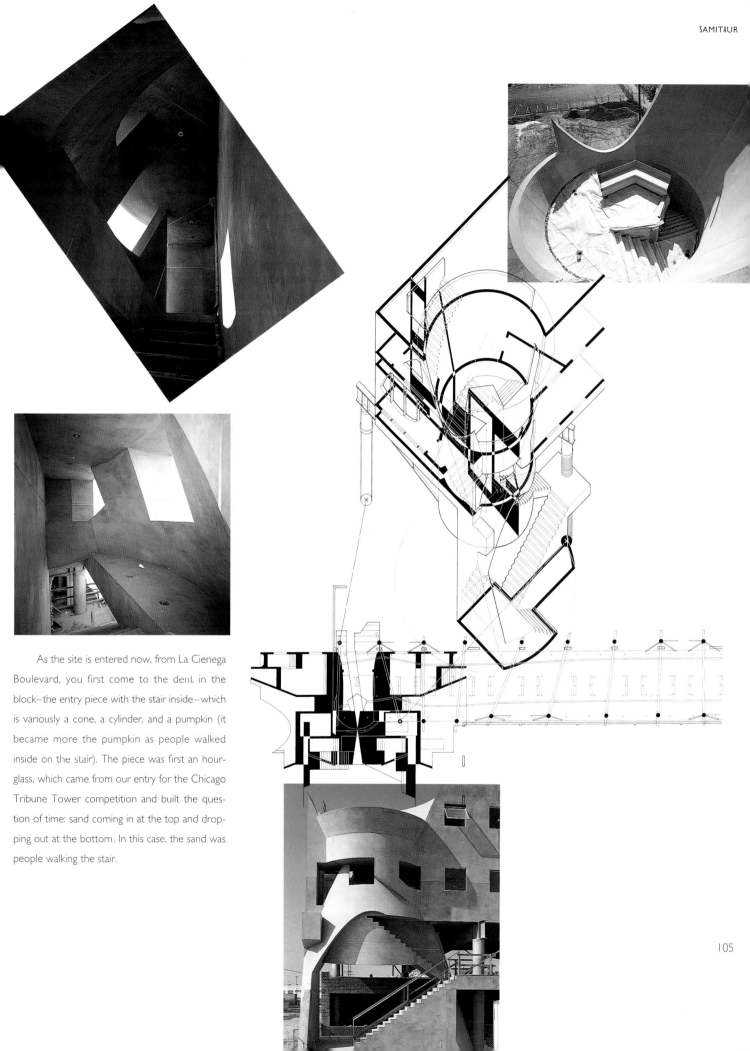

As the site is entered now, from La Cienega Boulevard, you first come to the dent in the block—the entry piece with the stair inside—which is variously a cone, a cylinder, and a pumpkin (it became more the pumpkin as people walked inside on the stair). The piece was first an hourglass, which came from our entry for the Chicago Tribune Tower competition and built the question of time: sand coming in at the top and dropping out at the bottom. In this case, the sand was people walking the stair.

Look at the girders underneath the block—every girder is the same and every girder is different. It's easy to resort to a technological exegesis—it looks like this because there's a rigid frame here; or we had to make this stiffener bigger; or the column is bigger in order to carry a bigger load. I'm suspicious of those explanations. Like the acoustic explanation of INCE THEATER: it's not completely untrue, but you know it's a cover for a different gambit.

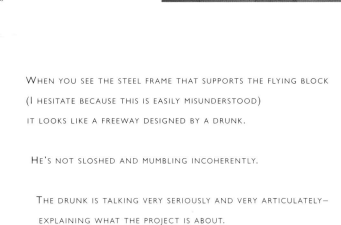

When you see the steel frame that supports the flying block
(I hesitate because this is easily misunderstood)
it looks like a freeway designed by a drunk.

He's not sloshed and mumbling incoherently.

The drunk is talking very seriously and very articulately—
explaining what the project is about.

But he's talking in a dream.

The drunk sees the world precisely, but very differently —
this is an argument for Coleridge and Xanadu.

Conventional analytical references are gone,
and a privatized version appears.

The other prominent indentation is the pool area, which is an admixture of two five-sided figures. That space, like the entry piece, has seating and stairs along with the pool. It's not a pool that fills up like a swimming pool—it's inverted. The water is very thin; it "sheet-flows" into a hole, disappears, and is pumped around again. When you're in the pool area, backed up against the pentagon wall, and it's sedate and safe, you can look out through these serrated, austere, and disciplined edges to the sea of South Central Los Angeles' battered industrial sheds.

The underside of the pool area is a part of an arched structure where colur the original order of the frame were remo that trucks could exit under the pool. The the egress point. Above, on the deck, is a over the pool. So it's a bridge over a bridg

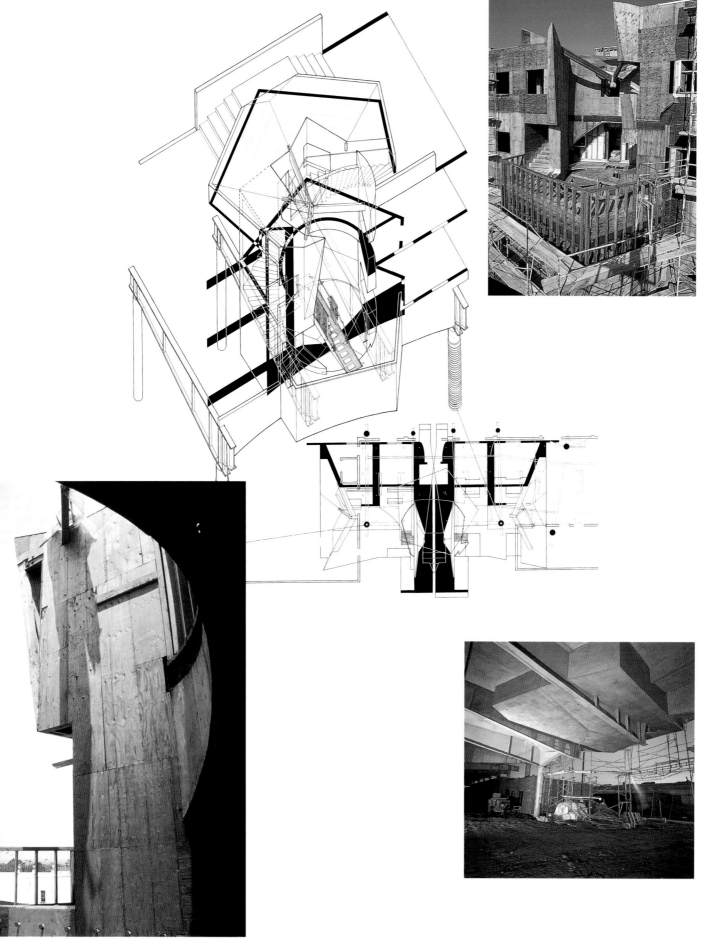

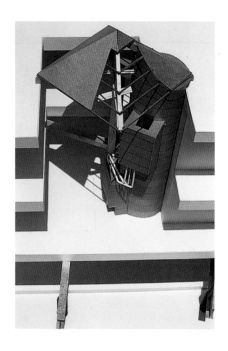

The other exception to the block is the boardroom, which hops up over the old saw-tooth roof. Go in the lobby, get on the elevator, and come up. If you go toward the cone, you're in the office space on two floors. Go the opposite way and there's a boardroom one-and-a-half floors in height that opens up to a remarkable view of Los Angeles: north to the Santa Monica mountains, east to downtown, and west to the beach along Wilshire Boulevard.

THIS IS AS POLITICAL A BUILDING AS YOU

COULD BUILD IN LA:

IT'S ADJACENT TO SOUTH CENTRAL LA

AND ITS SIZE IS OPTIMISTIC AND ASSERTIVE.

THE MANUFACTURING BASE ON THE GROUND WILL

REMAIN, BUT THE TYPE OF MANUFACTURING MAY CHANGE—

NOBODY KNOWS WHAT HAPPENS WHEN

YOU STICK OFFICES AND PRODUCTION IN THE AIR.

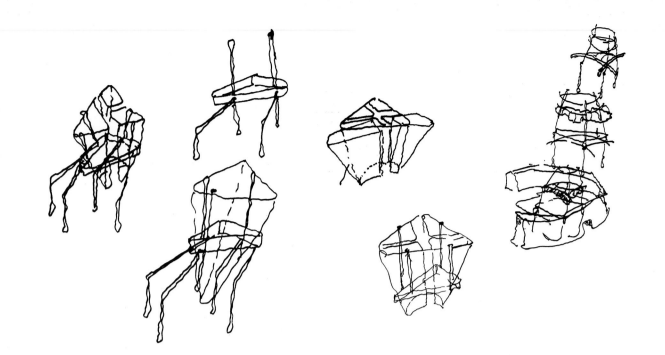

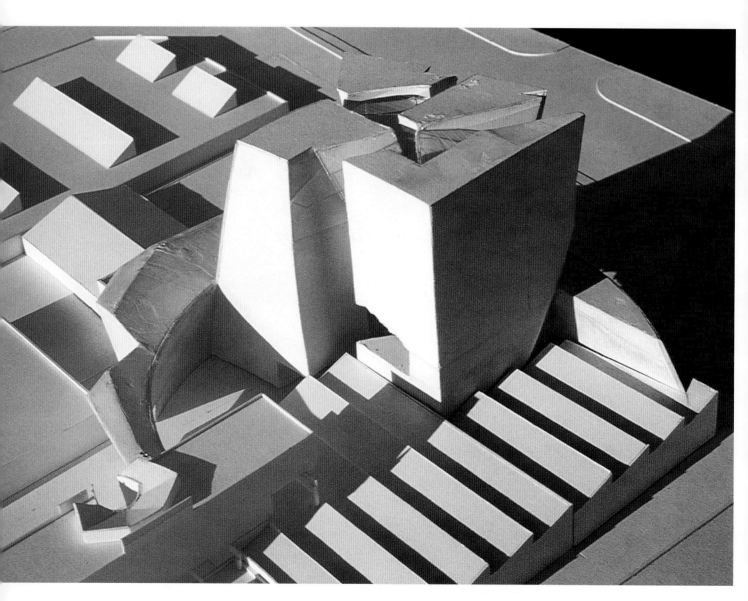

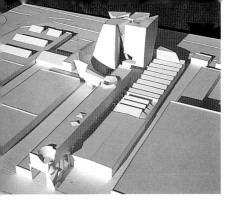

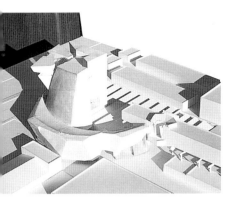

The second phase, which came a year or two after the first phase, is very much the extrovert. The first phase is the block in the air: see and be seen. The second phase is more covert: a plan hook creates an interior courtyard annex and attaches to phase one at the pentagon pool area.

While the first phase was under construction, the mayor's guys called and said, "Can you put another floor on Samitaur?" (Because they liked it.) And I said, "Well, you can't put another floor on the building because it'll fall down, but we have the Hook coming up." The Hook was originally designed to conform to the forty-eight-foot height limit. And they said, "Okay, can you take the second phase and redesign it so it clearly breaks the height limit?" So the erstwhile introverted second phase now has a tower 125 feet high.

The Hook could be first and then the Tower, but the way they're connected they should be done together. It's a steel frame, nine floors—which certainly jumps out of that landscape. It's very much a hypodermic, an emotive hypodermic to the area—positive and assertive.

The insertion of the block and the Hook in the neighborhood is never abetted by the bulldozer. I acknowledge the original organization of the buildings: some are left, some amended, some demolished. The area isn't sacrosanct, but it still has residual meaning: the new changes the old, but doesn't blot it out.

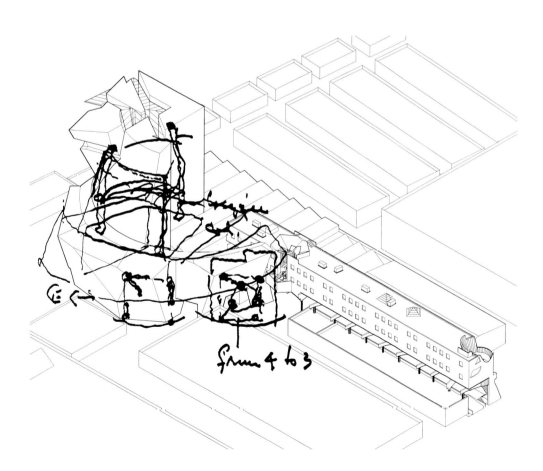

I CAN'T SEE CONSISTENTLY.

EVERYTIME I LOOK I SEE SOMETHING ELSE.

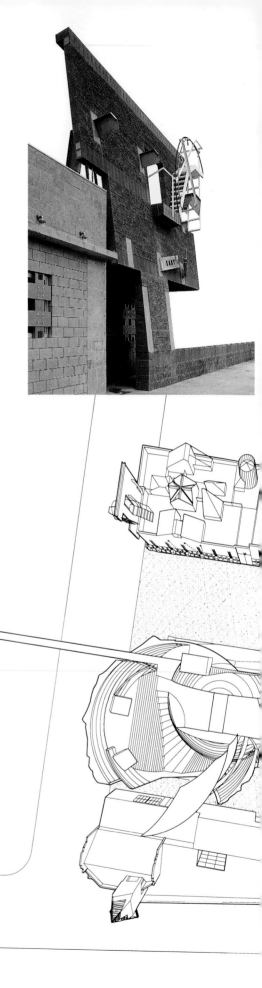

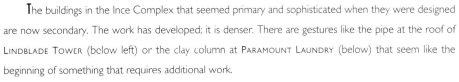

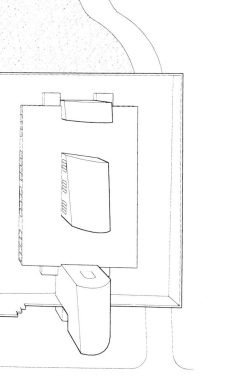

The buildings in the Ince Complex that seemed primary and sophisticated when they were designed are now secondary. The work has developed; it is denser. There are gestures like the pipe at the roof of LINDBLADE TOWER (below left) or the clay column at PARAMOUNT LAUNDRY (below) that seem like the beginning of something that requires additional work.

Sometimes this group of buildings is discussed as if it were anticipated originally that the four buildings would surround the theater. It's never that neat. The forecast is always reforecast. I did the first three buildings, one by one, without knowing whether we would get around to four (under construction), or five.

The current prediction is that the interior site will become a park. So the link between the four buildings—Paramount, Lindblade, GARY GROUP (above left), and METAFOR (above)—is grass. The parking lot drops below grade. Across Lindblade, Sony is building new offices and a parking structure.

The INCE THEATER (middle left) in the park is the east terminus of the redevelopment of Culver City. The redevelopment widens sidewalks, closes streets, builds parks, and provides low-interest loans to refurbish local businesses—all positive, but a little prosaic in city planning terms. The theater should be a hypodermic to the new downtown.

INCE THEATER

CULVER CITY CA

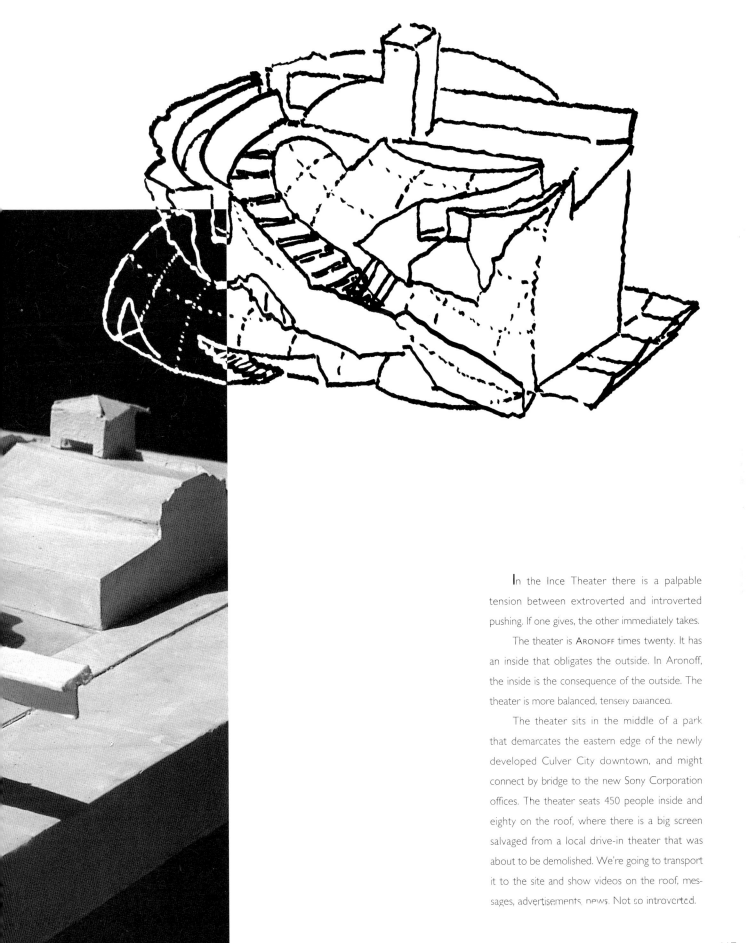

In the Ince Theater there is a palpable tension between extroverted and introverted pushing. If one gives, the other immediately takes.

The theater is ARONOFF times twenty. It has an inside that obligates the outside. In Aronoff, the inside is the consequence of the outside. The theater is more balanced, tensely balanced.

The theater sits in the middle of a park that demarcates the eastern edge of the newly developed Culver City downtown, and might connect by bridge to the new Sony Corporation offices. The theater seats 450 people inside and eighty on the roof, where there is a big screen salvaged from a local drive-in theater that was about to be demolished. We're going to transport it to the site and show videos on the roof, messages, advertisements, news. Not so introverted.

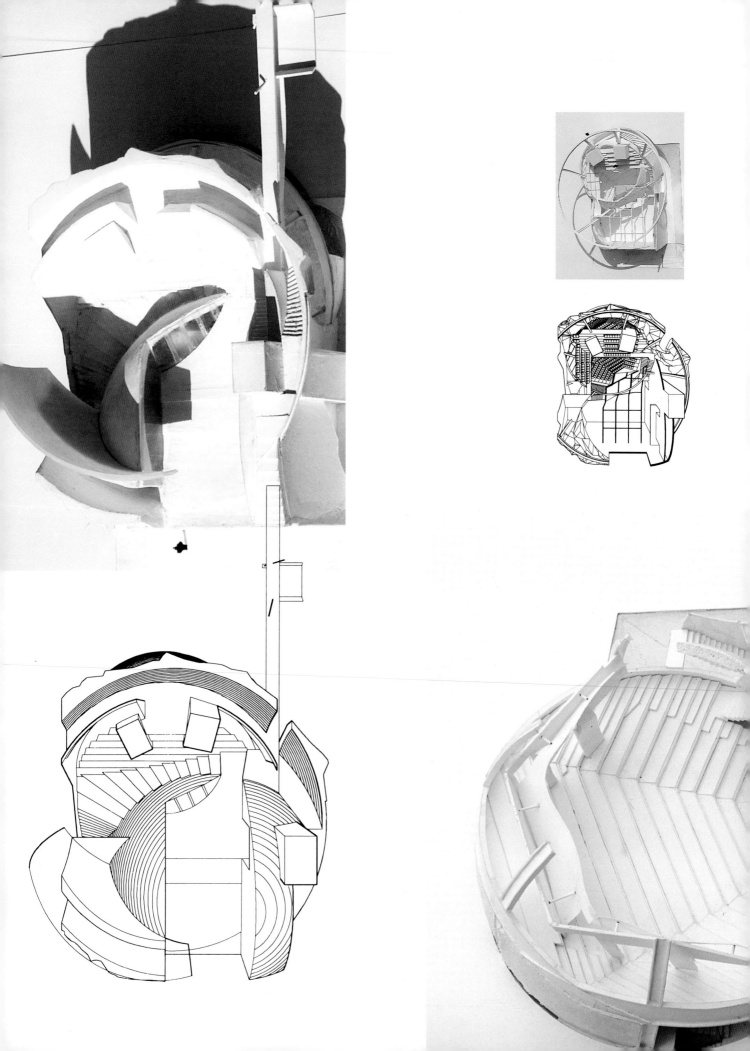

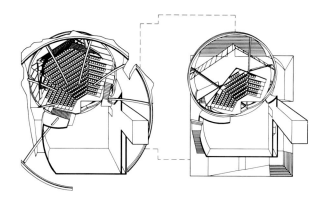

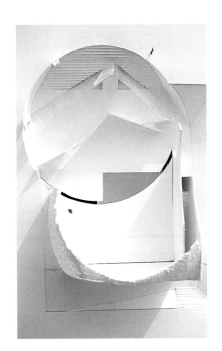

Conceptually the building is a duel not only between the obligations of inside and outside, but also between Pythagoras and his arch-enemy, but I don't know how to say who that is. Maybe the sound "om." How do you physically represent in architecture what can't even be circumscribed conceptually? So it's unrecognizable: the anti-3, 4, 5 triangle. It's anti-Euclidean, anti-system/quantity/ measure. Pythagoras grows out of the limitless and disappears back into the formless.

Here there are pieces of three spheres: the exterior at the top is a ruptured surface, nominally for acoustical reasons. From the ground you can see, but not hear, what's going on in the roof theater. It's isolated sonically. The technical-acoustical argument came retrospectively, after the decision to obligate that surface as the antithesis of the sphere. Another acoustical wall obviates the spheres inside. So there are two "oms," disingenuously related to the transmission of sound, that contest conceptual primacy with the spheres.

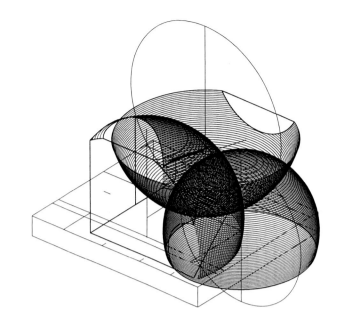

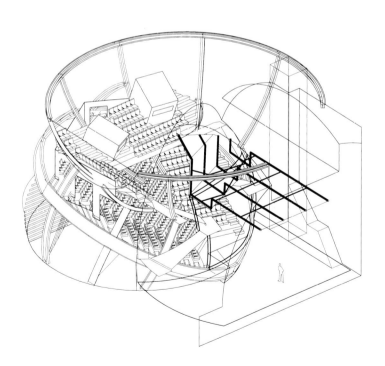

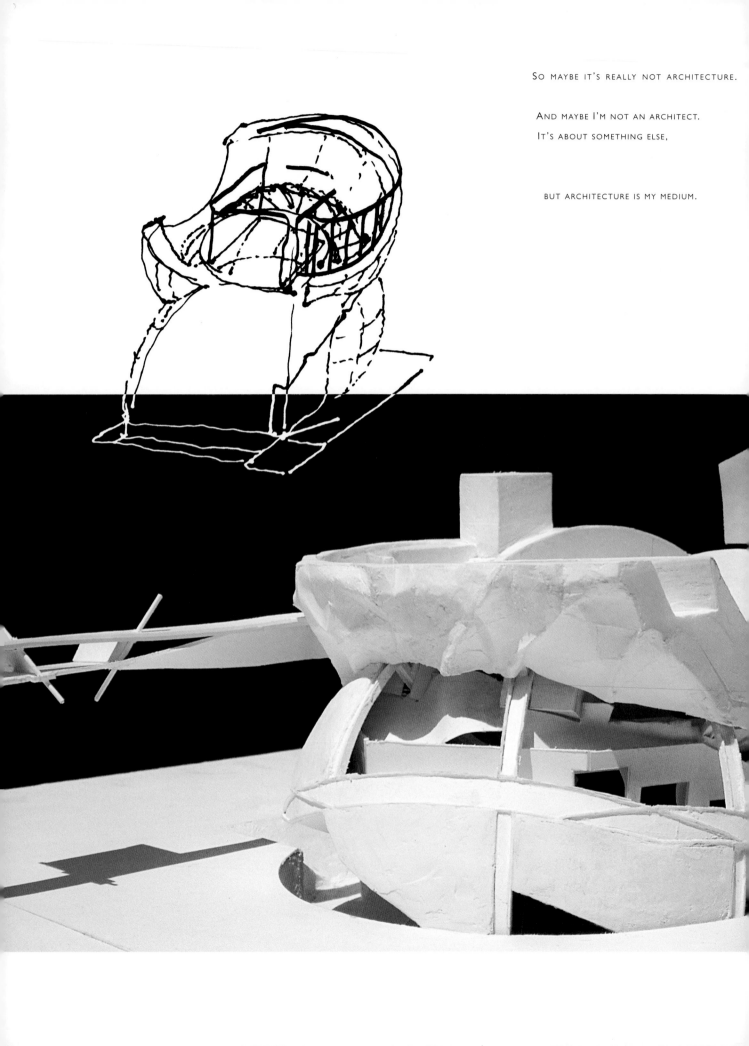

SO MAYBE IT'S REALLY NOT ARCHITECTURE.

AND MAYBE I'M NOT AN ARCHITECT.
IT'S ABOUT SOMETHING ELSE,

BUT ARCHITECTURE IS MY MEDIUM.

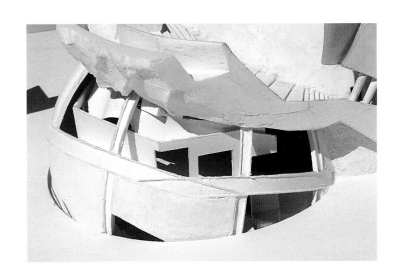

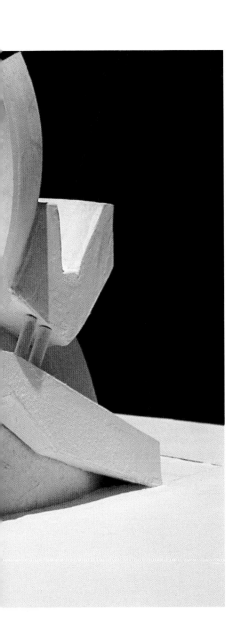

The theater manifests the GARY GROUP hypothesis: you might get to the truth-as-contradiction by stretching the extremes, but by not insisting on either end. Interesting that STEALTH insists on the ends—does it get at the truth?

This project is a transmutation to built form of a felt condition in me. That condition underlies what you see, how I understand, and the building is a way of putting that down.

The way to understand the big steel beam that wraps around the sphere is that it is not a circumference. The beam follows the seating profile; it doesn't conform to the sphere's regular geometry. Then there are secondary ribs, columns/beams, that conform to the curve of the sphere, perpendicular to the major ring beams. So the secondary beams depend on the geometry of both the sphere and the rings, which depend on pragmatic, internal circumstances. As the rings change position, so do the secondary supports, which have right angle obligations to the rings.

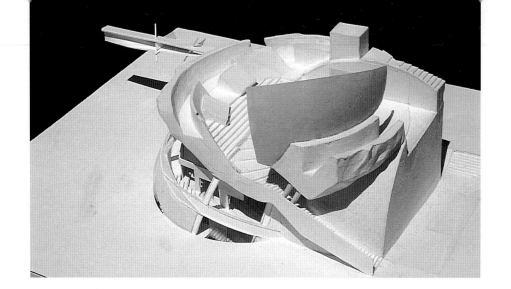

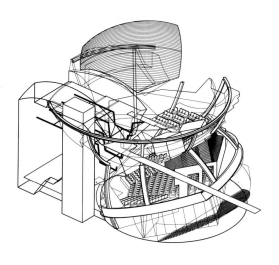

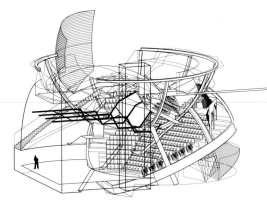

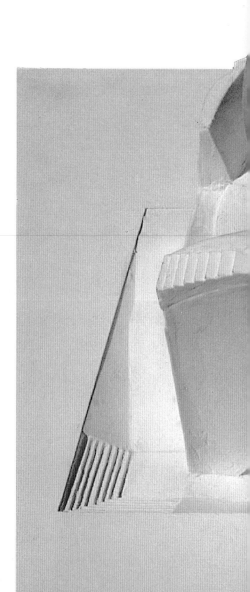

The Ince Theater stretches the spatial prospect. To accomplish that I had to break out of whatever constraints exist in formulating any recognizable geometry. I had to find a way to build geometric antithesis. Somebody called this conflict Dionysian versus Apollonian. Apollo is cerebral, but Dionysus is supposed to exist outside the intellect. In my case, both gods are cerebral, but the Dionysus/Apollo conflict is an accurate forecast of my sensibility.

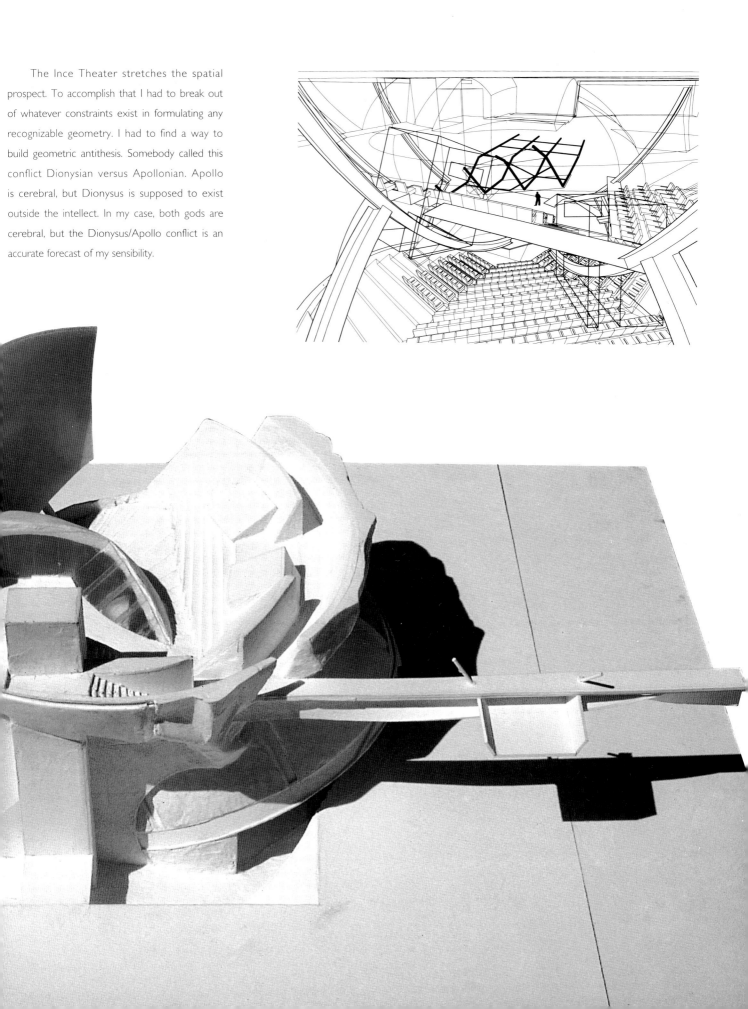

METAFOR

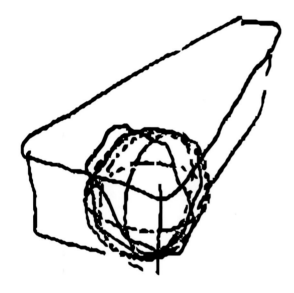

Metafor was designed about the same time as GARY GROUP. The original shed is trapezoidal in plan, with the anomaly positioned in the corner to maximize its impact on the entrance and the street. This object has its own form(s)—twelve-sided, and a sphere—and also subtends the acute plan angle and the vaulted roof of the original building.

The sphere appears for an instant as a cut in the concrete at the top of the Gary Group wall extension. Then, around the corner on Poinsettia, the sphere appears again, a very large curved (and angled) cut that opens the wall to the street. And on the roof, a curving steel trough is the physical edge of the mostly ethereal sphere. These wall and roof openings are covered by glass that never fits. It's always too big for the aperture it covers.

126

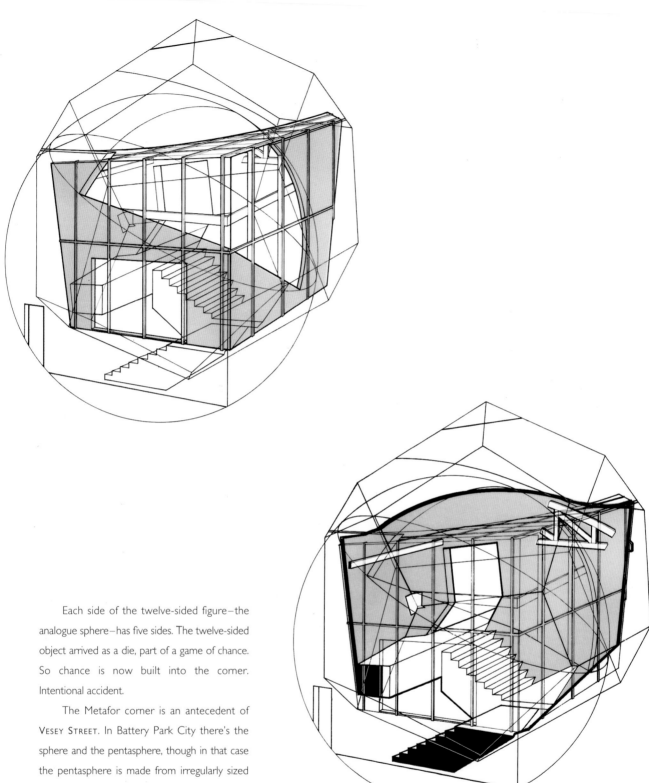

Each side of the twelve-sided figure—the analogue sphere—has five sides. The twelve-sided object arrived as a die, part of a game of chance. So chance is now built into the corner. Intentional accident.

The Metafor corner is an antecedent of VESEY STREET. In Battery Park City there's the sphere and the pentasphere, though in that case the pentasphere is made from irregularly sized five-sided pieces, as if the fabricator didn't quite know what a sphere was or how to go about constructing it.

When you enter the building you are inside the outside, but still outside the inside of the anomoly. From the lobby you see the erstwhile die enclosing the inside of the inside in the corner, where a stair connects to a second-level mezzanine. Inside the inside you get the die- and sphere-generated cuts in the exterior concrete walls. What's left of the twelve-sided die and sphere wraps around you. And the "too-big" glass covers the wall and the roof holes up to the steel trough.

Inside the inside completes the relationship between in and out.

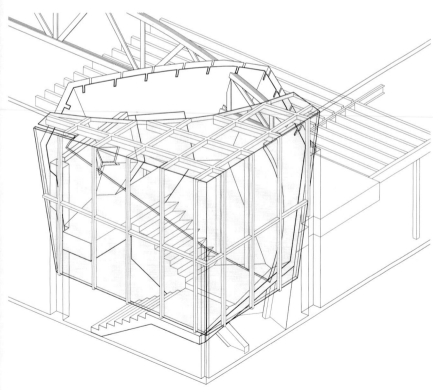

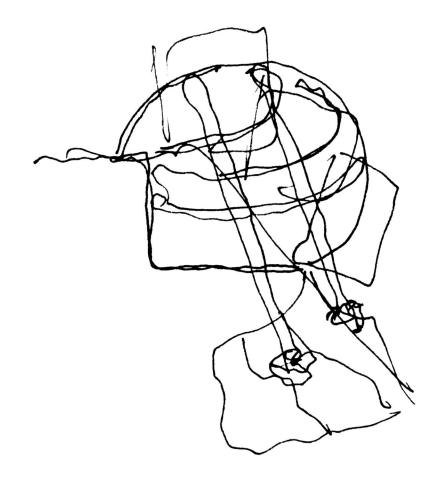

Two houses: On the flat portion of the site is a conventionally innocuous house. The north edge of the property slopes toward the north and west and can't be built on because it's owned by the Santa Monica Conservancy, whose job is to buy up land and keep it for the virtuous few.

The guest house sits on the flat-to-slope transition. I placed the sphere at the edge of the hill. Why is that germane? In the GARY GROUP it's the wall that leans yet doesn't. In a recent lecture I used a Degas ballerina to illustrate an asymptotic relationship, balance to imbalance. That's the feeling in Aronoff. The sphere is the essence of the building, but when you arrive it's almost hidden by the orthogonal entry face.

The sphere is alive—it disappears, reappears, and cuts the land. I never resolved how that cut would be represented materially. Poured? I don't think so. It will probably be horticulture with an almost spherical configuration; not precise, but not so ambiguous that you would lose the partial ball cut into the earth.

137

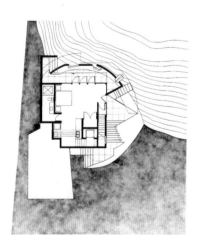
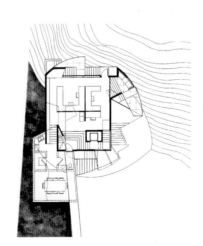
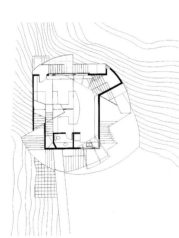

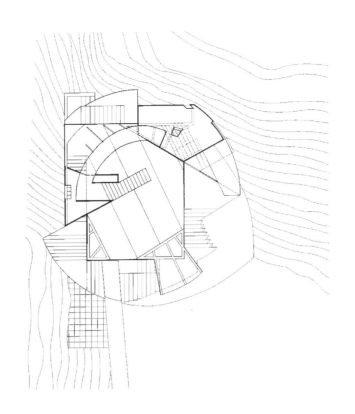

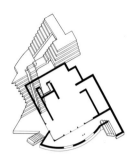

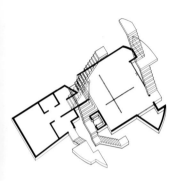

When I talked to the clients, there were programmatic concerns about connecting this to this and that to that. The discussion was resolved by allowing everybody to go almost everywhere. It's a toy, a tactile toy; you can climb all over the thing.

I make something that might roll, and then build into it qualities that counter the rolling. There's the prospect of motion, but the curved surface is made of orthogonal blocks. Tough to roll a block. I could strengthen the ball.

My best projects are balanced between the exchanging pressures of internal and external forces. I need the tension as a hypothesis. In Aronoff, outside controls. Inside is more accommodation. Aronoff, the extrovert; LAWSON/WESTEN, the introvert.

I'm interested in Henry Moore's *Helmet* series, beautiful and compelling. A great exegesis for the aesthetic strategy in Aronoff. You don't understand the helmet from the inside unless you take a chain saw to it.

THE AESTHETIC RESOLUTION ISN'T HOMOGENEOUS; IT'S A HETEROGENEOUS SYNTHESIS.

THE BUILDING IS AN INTENDED OXYMORON.

IT COULD BE ALL BALL. BUT IT'S NOT.

VERY LITTLE OF IT IS BALL.

I WANT AN INTELLECTUAL CONFLICT, LYRICALLY RESOLVED.

A FREEHAND SPHERE.

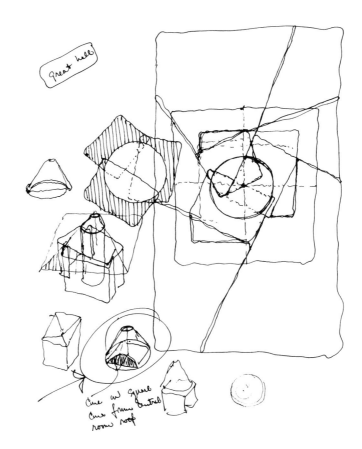

This house is a geometric hybrid. As the individual components are gathered, their legibility disappears in a force-field of obligations to the bigger object. New components appear, introducing strategies that are apart from the rules of geometric parts.

The hybridized geometry starts with the plan center of the site. In the earliest stages of the project I made a sketch that became WARNER THEATER, an interpenetration of three identical solids. Then came the cylinder with the center off-center, and the cone on-center, and the inter-working of the two. Then the cone was cut and circumscribed by a square.

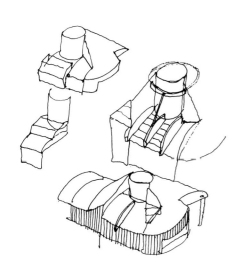

BY GOING SOMEWHERE, I PRECLUDE

SOMEWHERE ELSE. THE BEAM IS AN

EFFORT TO HOLD ON TO BOTH.

I WANTED TO INDICATE THE

POSSIBILITY THAT I COULD HAVE

GONE ELSEWHERE.

A vertical slice through the cone produced a parabolic curve. I grabbed the curve and yanked east. That's the vault. It's not the whole vault because the cone isn't the whole cone, since it was delimited by the square. So the parabola is incomplete, the vault only a partial one. Supporting the vault is a beam that follows the parabolic curve on top and is faceted underneath: a piece of wood, two pieces of steel, another piece of wood. The beam appears piecemeal: you never get a complete beam supporting the vault. If I had cut the section through the entire cone, the whole beam would be there to support it. Only one beam at the entrance, hanging way out, describes the full extent of the cut. So this beam is the residue of what might have been. I could have done this and gone there. Alternate avenues. I can't go everywhere.

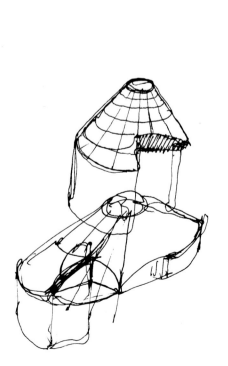

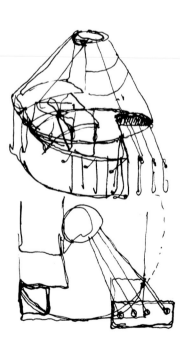

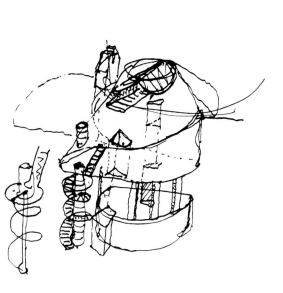

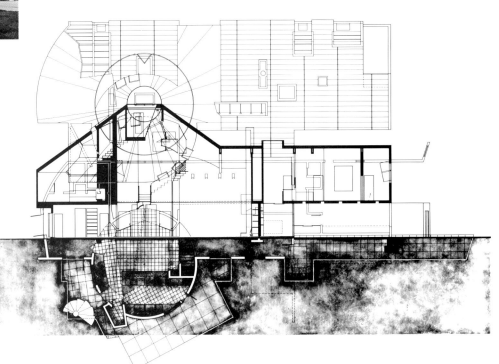

The cylinder and the cone have different centers. The cone is the center of the site. The cylinder adjusts to accommodate it. A steel ring, concentric with the cone, goes outside the north wall of the cylinder. The ring shows up on the inside and supports the wood framing of the cyli-cone roof. There are nine pipe columns, equidistant from one another around the cylinder. One appears on the first level, two on the second. The rest are hidden. Three steel girders connect the columns.

You're on the first floor: Girders fly above, bridging the space—one supports a second-floor walkway, another the third-floor mezzanine, another the fourth-floor deck. The pipes sit on girders and support the steel ring. The steel bridges carry no one to nowhere.

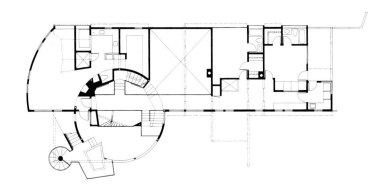

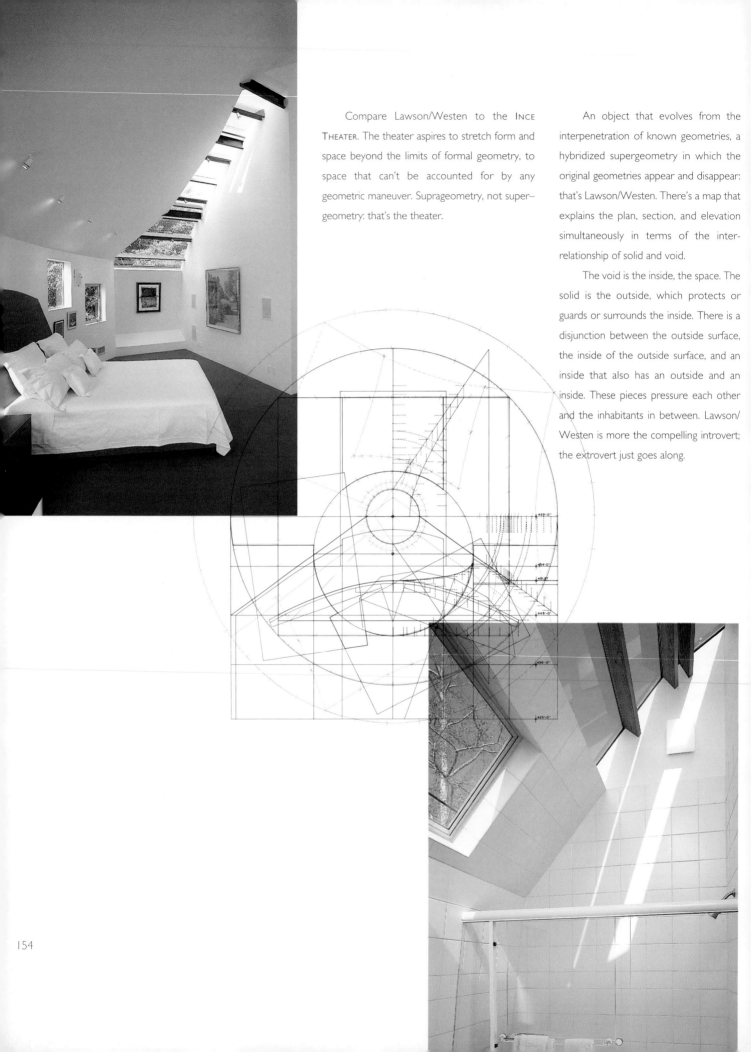

Compare Lawson/Westen to the INCE THEATER. The theater aspires to stretch form and space beyond the limits of formal geometry, to space that can't be accounted for by any geometric maneuver. Suprageometry, not super–geometry: that's the theater.

An object that evolves from the interpenetration of known geometries, a hybridized supergeometry in which the original geometries appear and disappear: that's Lawson/Westen. There's a map that explains the plan, section, and elevation simultaneously in terms of the inter-relationship of solid and void.

The void is the inside, the space. The solid is the outside, which protects or guards or surrounds the inside. There is a disjunction between the outside surface, the inside of the outside surface, and an inside that also has an outside and an inside. These pieces pressure each other and the inhabitants in between. Lawson/ Westen is more the compelling introvert; the extrovert just goes along.

There's a varying density of insides. The vault is lower in density; it is derivative, both conceptually because there are lots of vaults, and specifically and idiosyncratically because it belongs to an operation on the cone-roof. The main space—I never knew how to name it, so it's simply the high-rise kitchen—is implosion. The antecedent has priority. The vault couldn't surpass its progenitor, the kitchen.

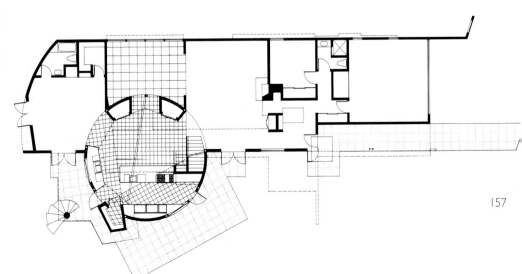

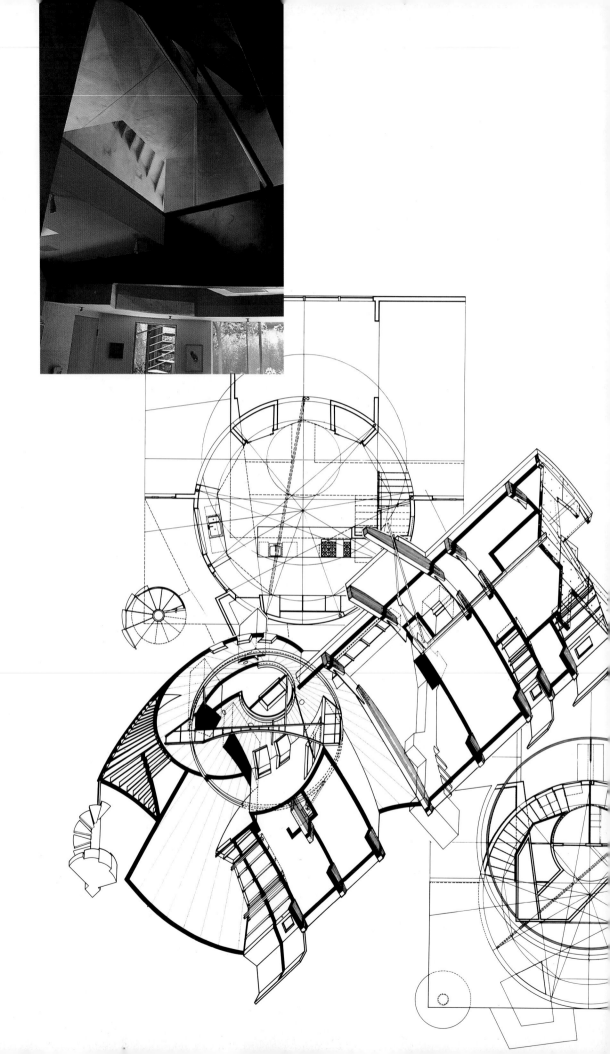

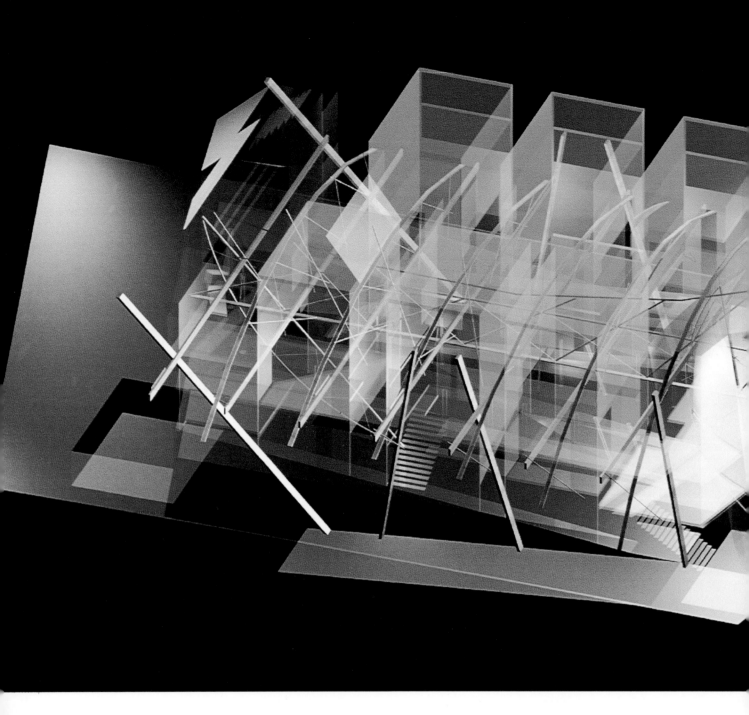

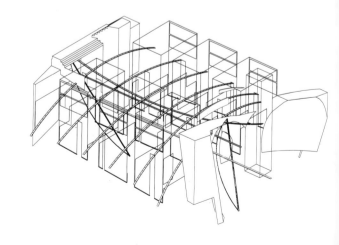

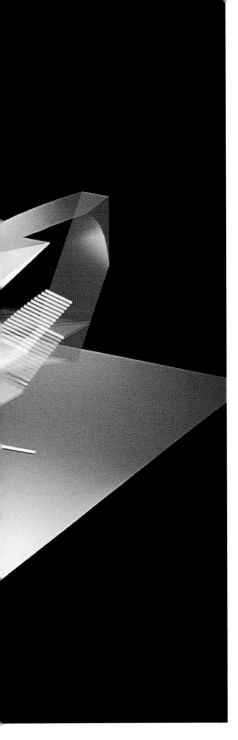

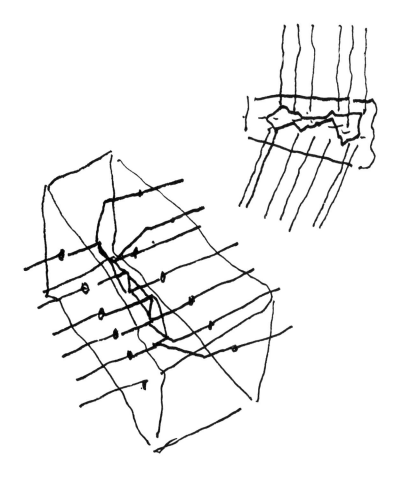

What I learned from working on the R Series is particularly applicable to Ibiza. That series was really a critique of the conventional methodology for making decisions relating structure to use. The choice of a structural system is erroneous if based on a correlation between use and span-length. The spatial nonsequiturs in Psf were instigated by the need for the steel frame to climb over the original trusses. The expansive, high space is a consequence of accommodating the previous building. Jumping over and around the bowstring trusses results in consistently atypical offices. Ibiza takes this spatial accident and makes it intentional.

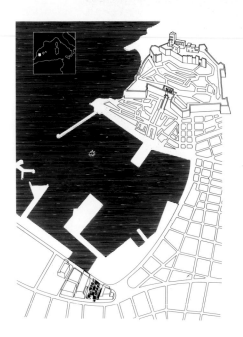

When the priest who owns the site talked about what he wanted in the building, I listened carefully and began by designing something quite different. As if, for instance, he had told me to make a jail and I said, "OK, I'LL MAKE YOU A JAIL," AND THEN I MADE HIM A HOSPITAL; AND WHEN I WAS DONE

MAKING HIM THE HOSPITAL I SAID,

The consequence of designing the hospital (which nobody asked for) gives the client an extraordinary jail that never would have been conceived if the original jail premise had simply been accepted. The idea with the Ibiza project was to go off in an opposite direction involving conceptual parts and ideas about the city that had nothing to do necessarily with the building's momentary utility.

"NOW THAT I'VE MADE YOU A HOSPITAL

I'LL TURN IT INTO A JAIL."

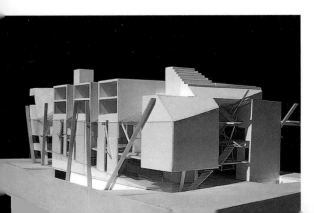

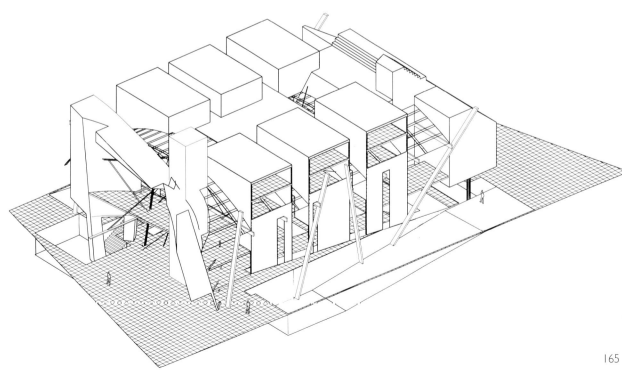

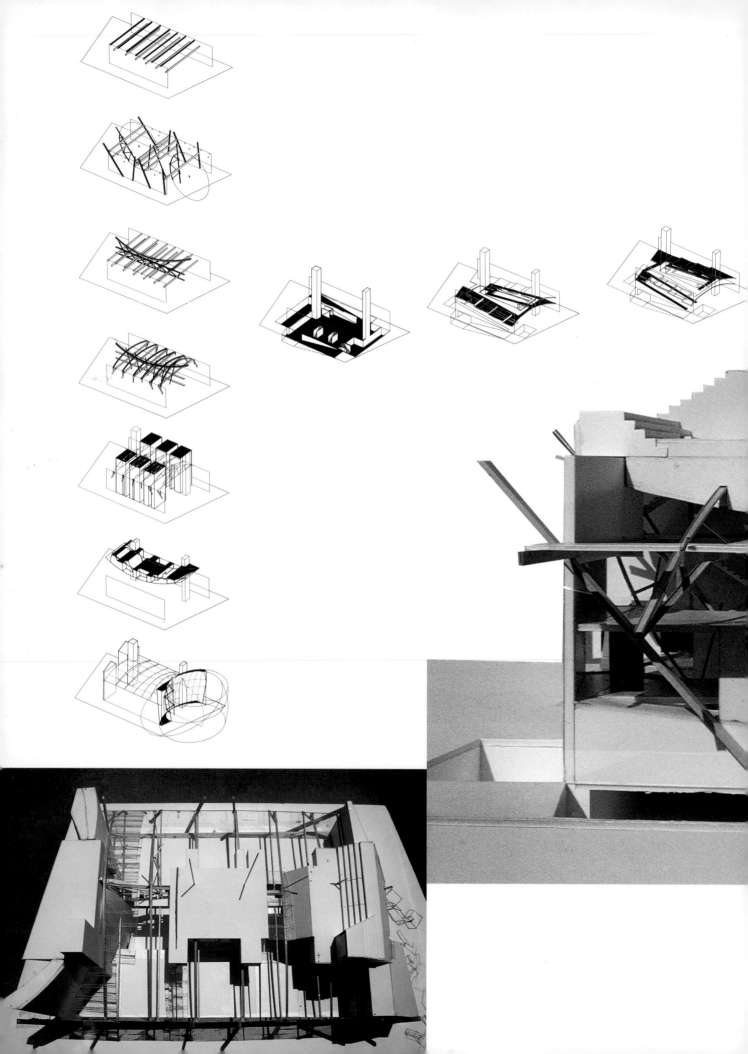

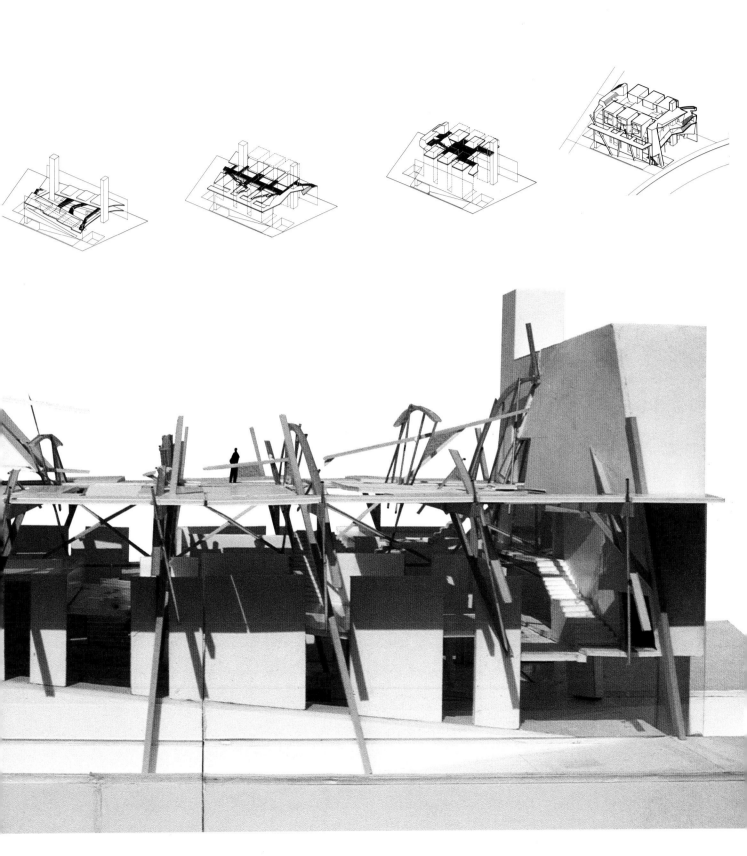

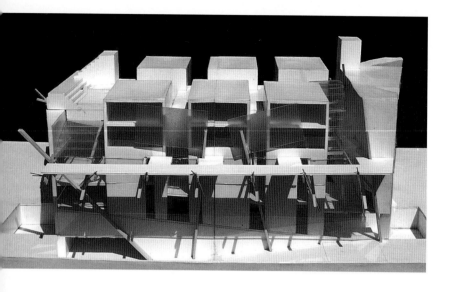

Part of this had to do with the perspective on history that I got by looking across the port at the old Renaissance city, a Roman necropolis, pieces of Carthage, and Muslim contributions, and realizing how ephemeral a building's use really is over time. Living, working, being operated on, being imprisoned, singing, dancing, loving, exhibiting: all these activities could take place in a structure whose form was originated with other uses in mind. Ibiza's visible pedigree pushed me in that direction: Make something of consequence in the context of a Roman necropolis, not in the context of Company A wanting to sell Product Z in the building. When Company A goes in the tank, a space will still precede and outlast it. The idea is to design a building that precedes and outlasts its temporal use.

168

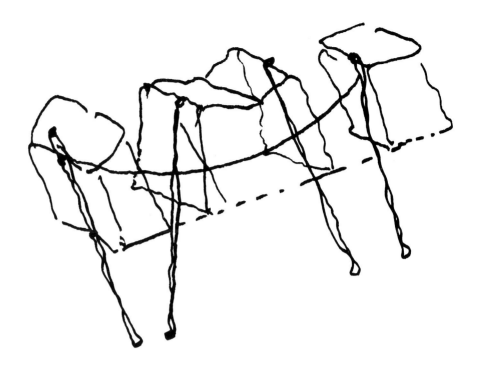

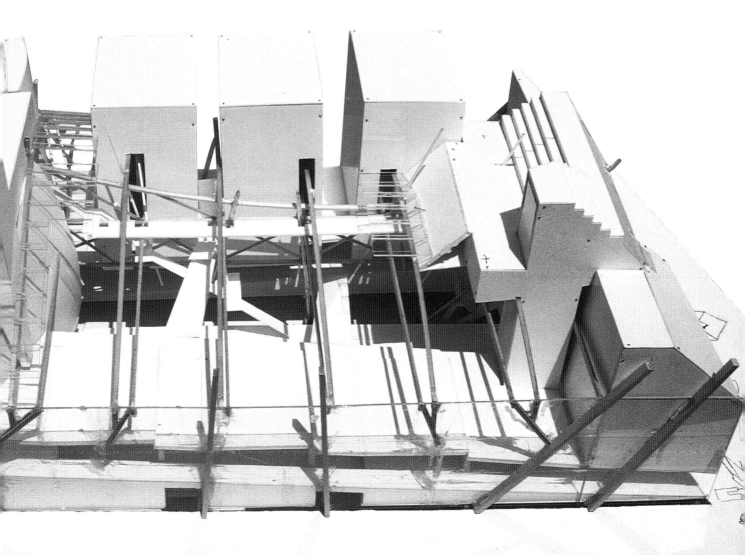

NARA CONVENTION CENTER

NARA JAPAN

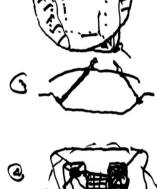

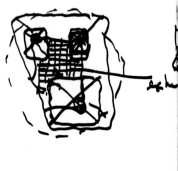

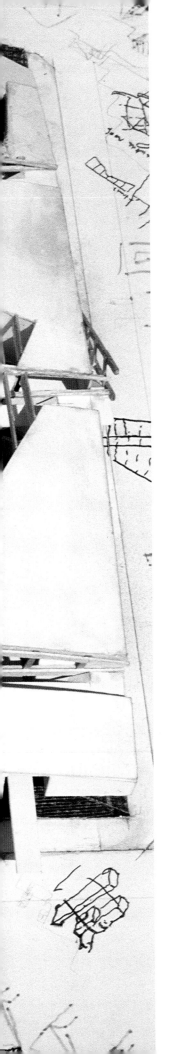

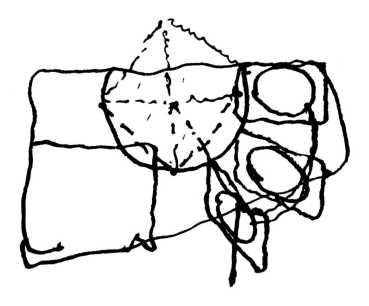

Nara was a trading center, the end of the old silk route, and an important religious center going back hundreds of years. I located a center for the triangular site that became the center of a partial sphere delimited by the sides of the triangle. The sphere is lifted on huge legs over a cut in the earth.

The top of the structure originates in the sphere and has a long-span structure carried to the ground on the legs of the three theaters. In the roof building, a series of trusses placed orthogonally repeats the old city street pattern. Each truss is like a comb: prescribed by the sphere in section and the grid in plan. You walk through the combs on the analogue grid. The trusses remind me of the roofs at Uxmal, particularly the Nunnery—no intrinsic relation to Nara, but a reference in my head.

EARLIER CULTURES CUT THE LAND TO INDELIBLY DEMARCATE

THEIR RELATIONSHIP TO THE EARTH'S SURFACE. THIS EARTH CUT IS PERSONAL.

171

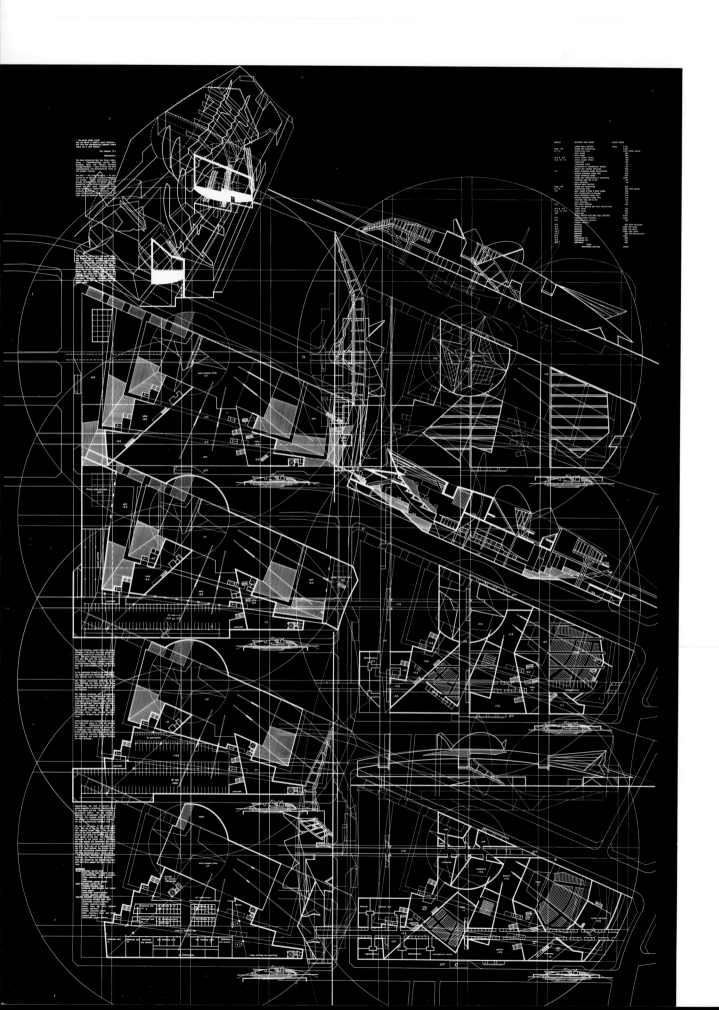

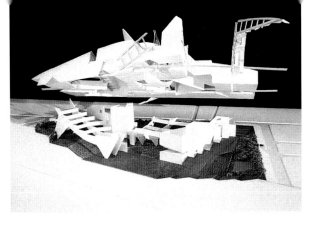

Together the building parts make an elemental poem: there's the cut earth; the curved lid, an analogue to the sky; and the theaters as bridges that connect land and sky. It's plausible for someone to experience the building and understand without the earth/bridge/sky exegesis; perhaps it's parenthetical. But that's the way I was thinking.

The elevations of the elevator and lobby blocks originate in a parabolic curve derived from the theater seating profile. There's a loose truss arm that connects to the train station across the street.

The convention center posits the sphere while acknowledging the grid; makes a center in a heretofore neutral field. But the truss grid isn't literally coincident with the immediate site, so the grid-within-the-sphere is a generic, not perceivable reference to the local street pattern.

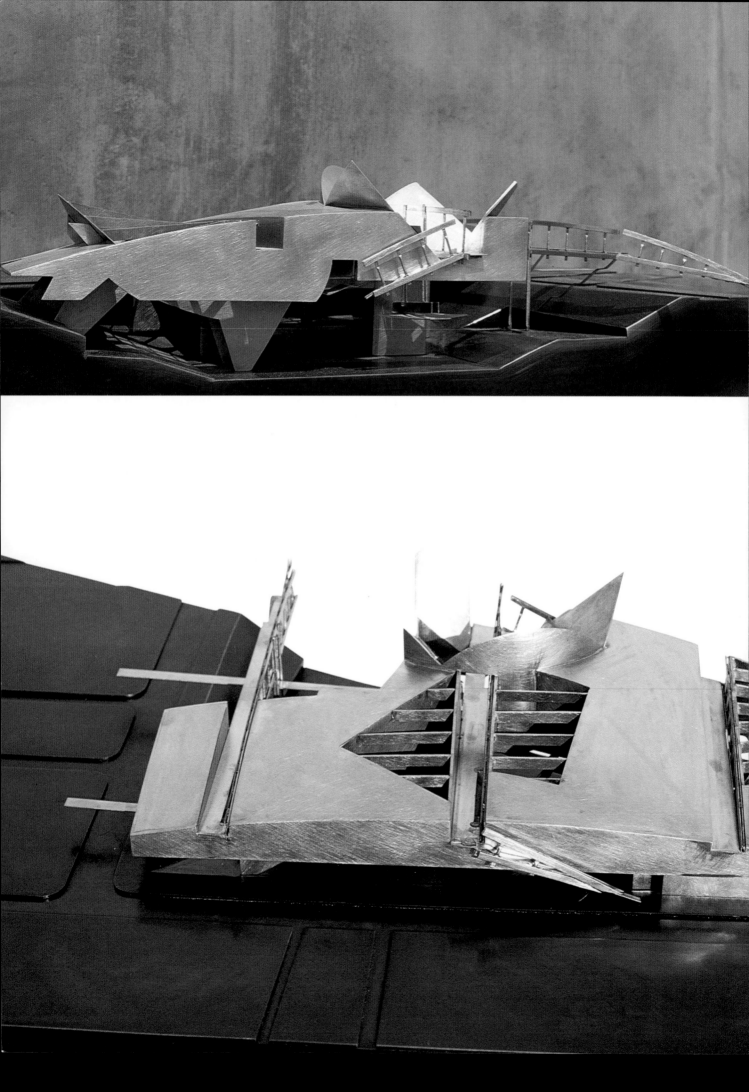

I REMEMBER SAYING TO MY DAUGHTER WHEN SHE WAS MAKING CHOCOLATE PUDDING

THAT IF YOU STIRRED IT ONE WAY

YOU WOULD COOK IT,

AND IF YOU STIRRED IT THE OTHER WAY

YOU WOULD UNCOOK IT.

AND SHE LAUGHED.

SHE STIRRED IT THE OTHER WAY AND IT STAYED COOKED.

YOU CAN'T UNCOOK NARA, EITHER.

THE PARTS ARE TOO INTERTWINED AND THEY'VE GIVEN UP TOO MUCH OF THEMSELVES.

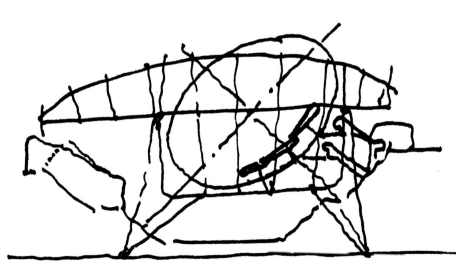

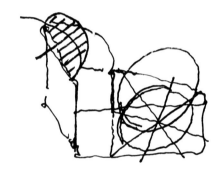

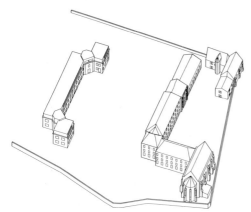

The literal and conceptual foundation for the Art Center is a dislocation and reconstitution of the site. The land is reformed as a series of contiguous, sloping grass plains, retained by masonry walls. The plains slope north to south and south to north, intersecting at an irregular valley that slopes west to east. The ruptured site produces a fresh landscape. Four new structures ride on the landscape.

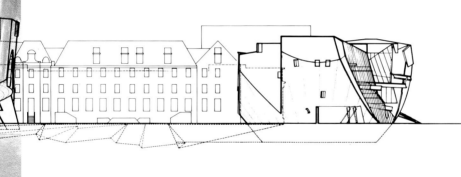
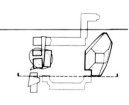

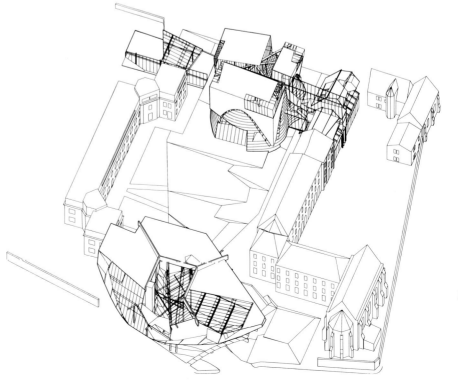

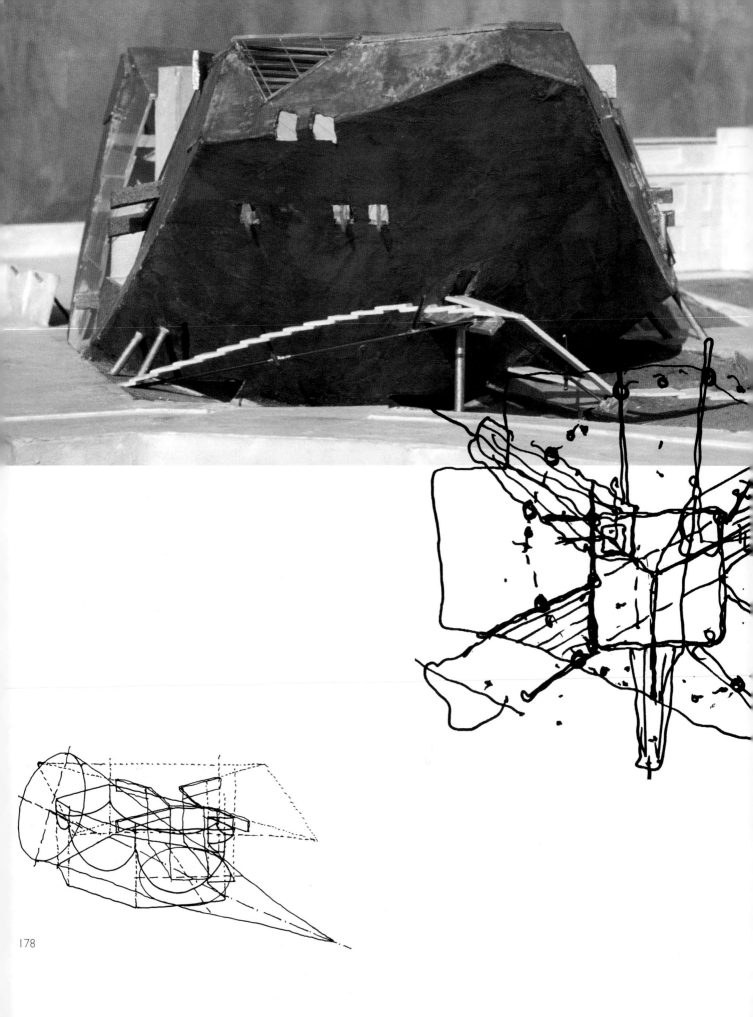

At the east end is the museum, which begins as a cone and tilts north toward the chapel and cinemas. A plain on an imagined property line slices the cone vertically. The cut volume within the property remains. The Euclidian origin is almost unrecognizable in the transformed object.

The museum is conceptually a spiral. Its floor varies in width as it rises clockwise around an orthogonal block that is square in plan and holds the cafe. The cafe block, on axis with the theater, projects vertically and governs the roof. Each of the three pieces of the roof slopes up or down from the building perimeter to one of the three cafe walls. The cafe roof is glazed, as is the east wall, which visually connects the cafe to the park. The top chords of hairpin trusses support the glass roof and carry the main floors. From the cafe, activity is visible on the floors above through glazed vertical slots in the interior walls. One truss chord passes through each slot.

The museum extends toward the historic city and defers to other existing circumstances. As a disingenuous act of architectural contrition, the east wall of the museum leans west, away from the park. The northwest wall frees itself from the corner of the current musicology/conservatory building by tilting east. A bridge flies across the face of the north wall, linking park and public garden.

The museum and the theater, in combination with the existing high school and musicology/conservatory, contain the new garden. The theater contains the site on the west and was designed in four steps. First, a cylinder was positioned vertically, squished, and attacked from the south (the high school) and north (the old conservatory). The squishing is another disingenuous deference to adjacent, existing buildings—an excuse to make the object.

The literal and conceptual foundation for the Art Center is a dislocation and reconstitution of the site. The land is reformed as a series of contiguous, sloping grass plains, retained by masonry walls. The plains slope north to south and south to north, intersecting at an irregular valley that slopes west to east. The ruptured site produces a fresh landscape. Four new structures ride on the landscape.

At the east end is the museum, which begins as a cone and tilts north toward the chapel and cinemas. A plain on an imagined property line slices the cone vertically. The cut volume within the property remains. The Euclidian origin is almost unrecognizable in the transformed object.

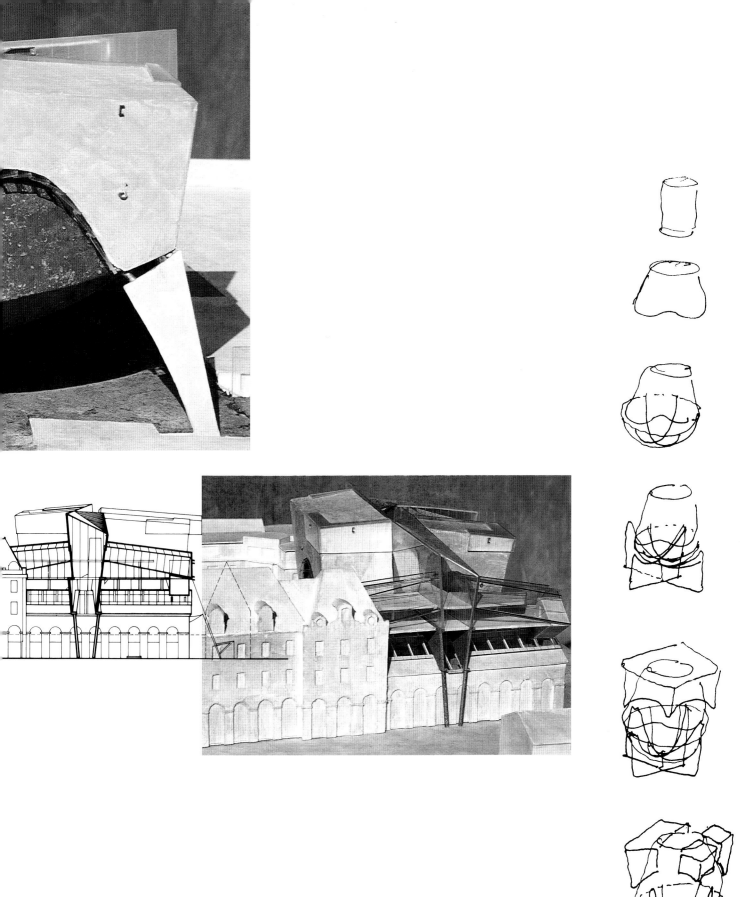

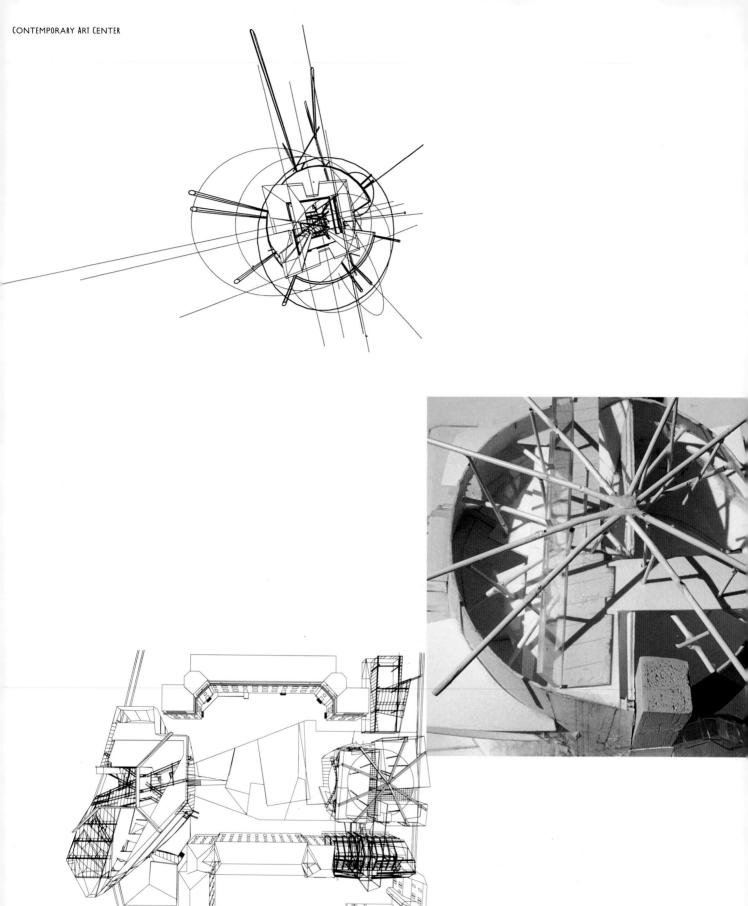

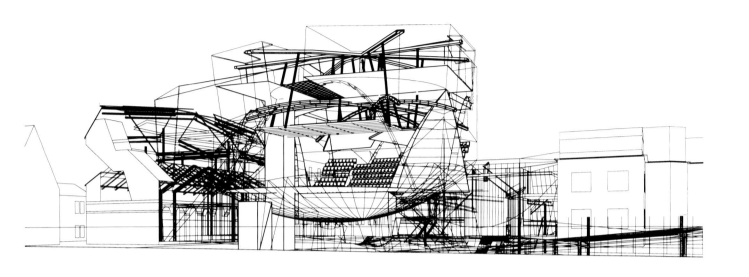

VLA has and is no name. Janet Saad-Cook, the artist who originated the project, and I didn't want to name it. We didn't want to say chapel or auditorium or gallery. When Ulysses put out the Cyclops's eye, the Cyclops said, Who are you? and Ulysses said, It's no-name. Ulysses was hiding his identity, his meaning. So are we.

Janet and I didn't want another Stonehenge or Caracol. Those early sites are now known to each other. They no longer exist in isolation, defining the relationship between a particular culture and the behavior of earth, sun, and moon at one location. Our intention is to build that astrocultural archaeology into this project more generically. We wanted to acknowledge other points on the earth where the sun behaves differently; a global, not local, updating of the Stonehenge idea.

There is a personal and cultural need to account for the behavior of earth and sky: what they did yesterday, and today, and will do tomorrow. This is not an empirical requirement, but something deeper, necessary to confirm intelligible meaning in a life. We don't want odd rocks hitting Jupiter—that makes everybody nervous.

I used to show Phobos, the Martian moon that rotates retrograde. (That's the wrong direction, assuming that MIT knows the right direction.) Phobos isn't spherical and it goes the wrong way. The scientists were wrong. Again. Where's the *where* where we're going? You say it's a road, has direction. Go six inches below the road and it's just dirt, so don't be so sure it goes where you think. Go down six inches and you have to start all over. This is the conceptual discussion that "no name" engenders.

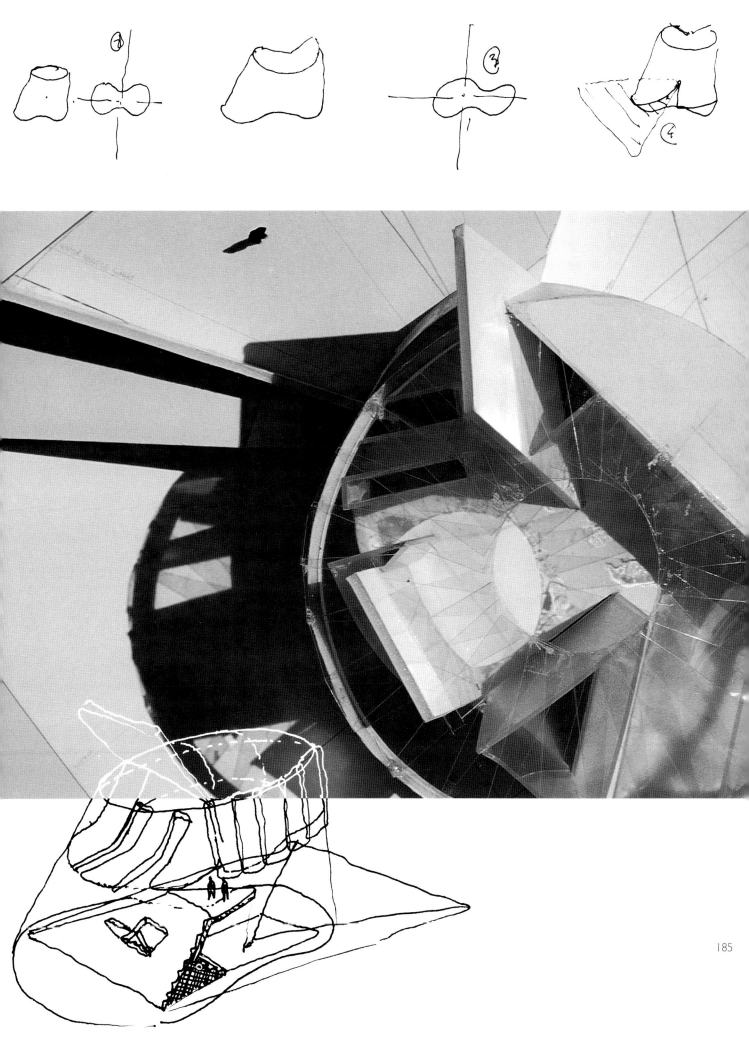

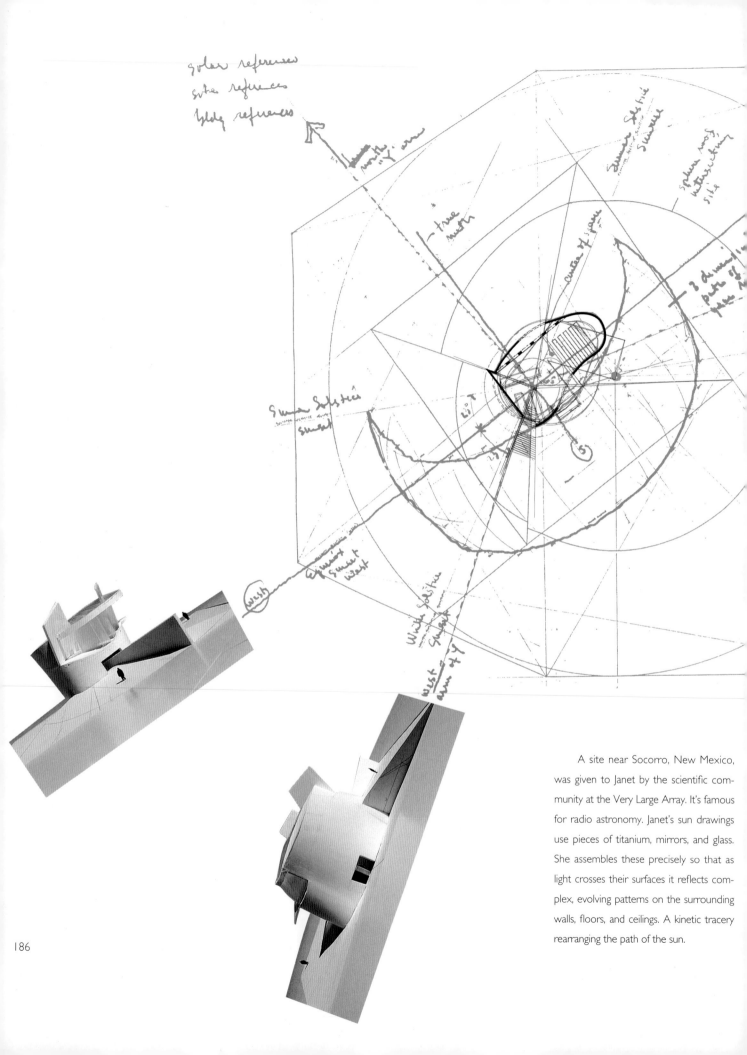

A site near Socorro, New Mexico, was given to Janet by the scientific community at the Very Large Array. It's famous for radio astronomy. Janet's sun drawings use pieces of titanium, mirrors, and glass. She assembles these precisely so that as light crosses their surfaces it reflects complex, evolving patterns on the surrounding walls, floors, and ceilings. A kinetic tracery rearranging the path of the sun.

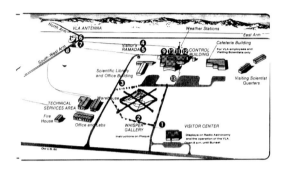

The VLA site is spectacular. Gargantuan apparatuses and three train tracks originate at a center. From there the tracks radiate 120 degrees apart from one another. The telescopes are placed on flatbed train cars and moved as earth and sky shift. In the midst of all this is the new building. It is not an auditorium, not a museum, not a gallery, not a chapel, but it will include aspects of all of them. You can look at the drawings and models and see that the volume is cut and perforated to let light instigate the sun drawings. There are a variety of apertures, and light comes through the roof. Janet's art is positioned high in the space, just below the roof, perhaps on arms, and the art delivers its patterns on the interior surfaces.

Squish a cylinder, push its face in. That's the first shape. Cut in magnetic north, true north, equinox, solstices. Take on walls, seats, stairs, doors. Insert the sun drawings. You enter from any of the four cardinal quadrants and sit on blocks. There are two floor levels: upper and lower. The high floor could be a speaker's podium. The main floor could hold an audience.

The surface of the squish deforms teleologically. "No-name" is directional and evolutionary.

187

The callig theory came from a poem that one of my students in New Haven gave me. The whole sequence is an accident. She's sitting in the studio practicing calligraphy and she paints the poem as an exercise. I ask her to explain. She says it's a five-hundred-year-old poem written by a woman whose husband left her. Despair. Image by image, the meaning of the poem is explained.

Calligraphy goes back to the origin of written language, a unity between image and concept. It's not auditory; it's not phonetic. Calligraphy can express a personal sensibility, the woman's grief, within a form-language that's suprapersonal. Cosmic order is intrinsic to calligraphy: the seasons, the sun and moon, the rivers. It is a conceptual, pictorial unity between one and many moving in and out of time. I remember the images that said that all the rivers flow east, and that spring would never come again in the poet's life.

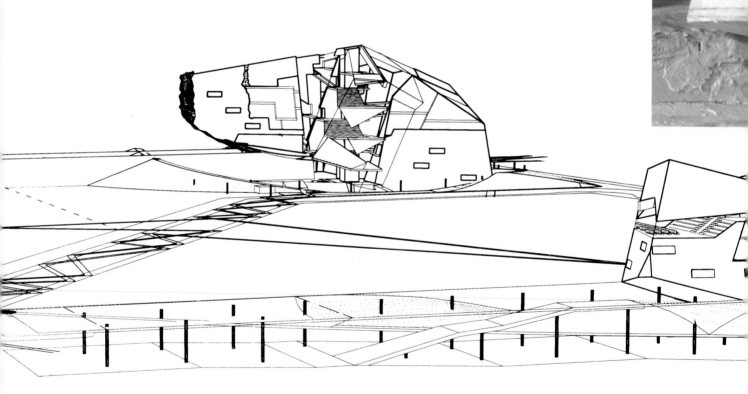

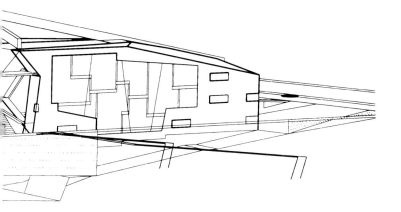

189

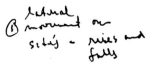

① lateral movement on
site's – rises and
falls

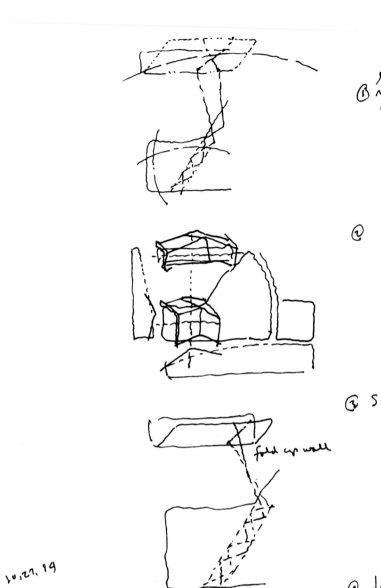

② height limits on
site (profiles)
roof forms (directional
roof cross axes

fold up wall

③ Sand mount
Ricochete
transister
water to
land

10.27.89

④ trees / sun
boxes – adjust south
and east

west

south

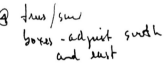

overlapping boxes
pierced by sky

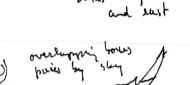

open

Calligraphy is aesthetic, not only in terms of how you see but how you think and feel and understand, because the form is elemental in the formation of culture and its associations with language. Calligraphy contains a structure that represents a coherent, intelligible world. Can architecture confirm that?

My aspiration was to develop an architectural calligraphy. The images would be outside the conventional architecture discussion. This calligraphy would be conceptual under the formal, implicating the formal. It could be exchangeable. Other architects would work on the project, picking up images and recombining them. I established the basic syntax of the project, but not only on my site. The calligraphy crosses all seven sites.

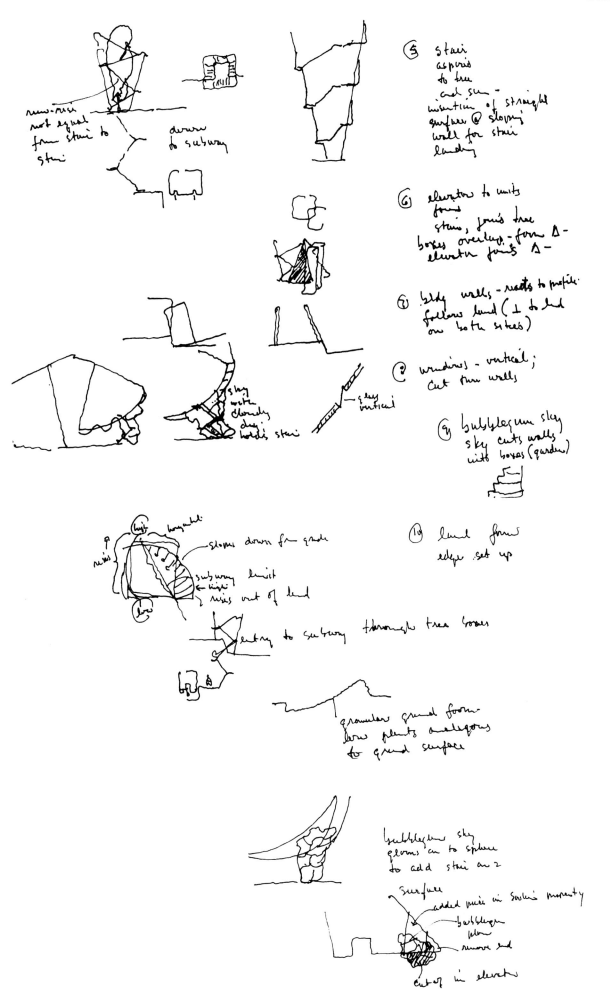

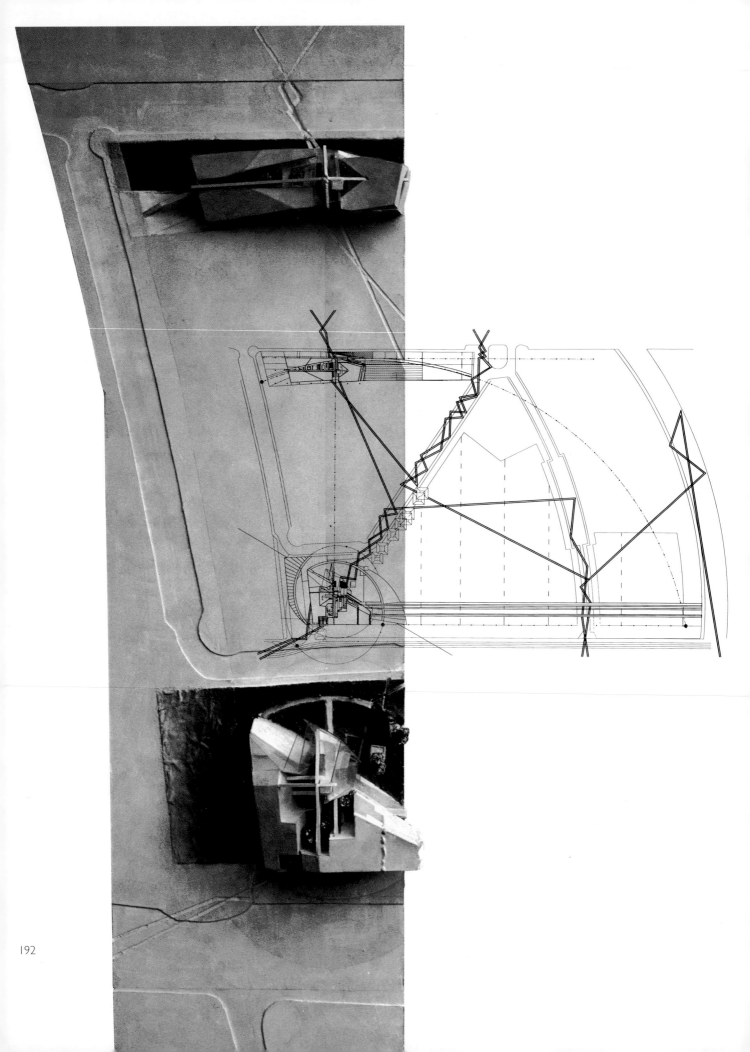

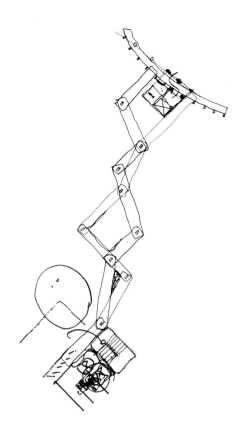

The question was, how to make the characters? The cosmological framework isn't really available to me. I liked the way the poem and its form-language were passed along and warped. My student misunderstood the poem, I misunderstood her, and the Viennese misunderstood me. But the idea moved across time and from one place to another: from China to New Haven to LA to Vienna. My characters can't be Mandarin, obviously. It is a private form, imposed by the architect. It's a language because I say so, but it also resonates outside of me.

The first move was to lift the SANDPIPER BRIDGE from an old project where it was attached and had a particular meaning. Now it's free. Has nothing to do with Vienna. The sandpiper is a long-legged bird that inhabits a narrow seashore zone between water and land. The neither/nor zone. The sandpiper callig is a transition between diverse conditions, an intermediary—not water, not earth, but both at once. That's the project sensibility, too.

In LA, the Sandpiper was never complete. Vienna took care of that. The Sandpiper was positioned along an existing walk running diagonally through the site to the corner of Wagramerstrasse. I looked at it not only in terms of form, but how the bird might move. If sandpipers really moved like this they'd be in trouble, but I called the Sandpiper's path the ricochet callig. The Sandpiper bounces off the walk's edges according to angles of incidence and reflection, like a ball on a pool table, leaving a trail, scratching the earth. The bird moves in plan and section. The motive of the diagram was to bounce the ricochet callig between my two sites, then on to others.

There are a lot of mature trees on the entire site, so the Viennese planners asked if I could protect the horticulture. Part of the original calligraphy has to do not only with a singular image/idea, but with additive modifications. So there's the tree, and ten trees, and a forest. From one to many.

The tree container is enlarged to the south and west to allow sunlight in. There are many trees together, so the aggregate is a sunlit garden. From tree to container to sun to garden. Then the garden opens up with walls, sometimes vertically straight, sometimes inclined, that follow the theoretical tree containers. The walls stretch across all the sites, parallel to the Wagramerstrasse, so everyone can walk to the garden. In the calligs, a stair is a vertical analogue for a tree. We don't conventionally correlate stair and tree, but in the callig, stair and tree share verticality.

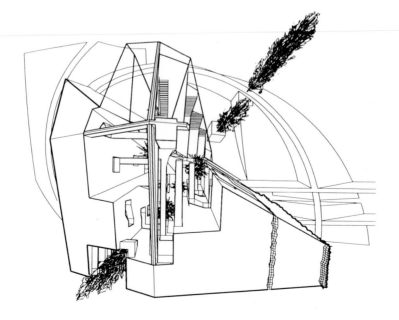

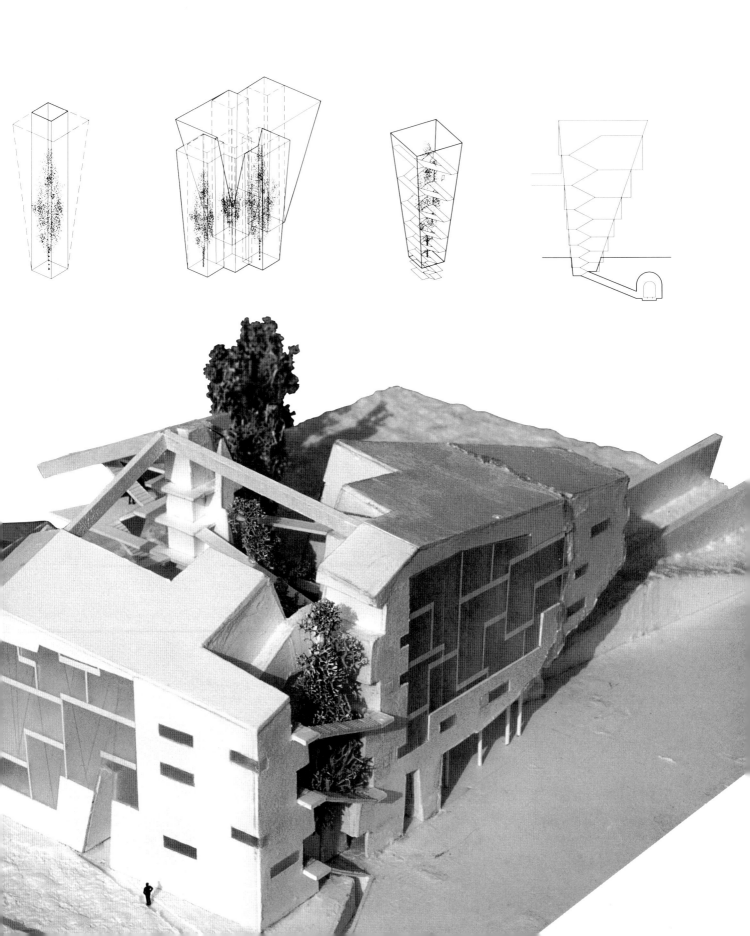

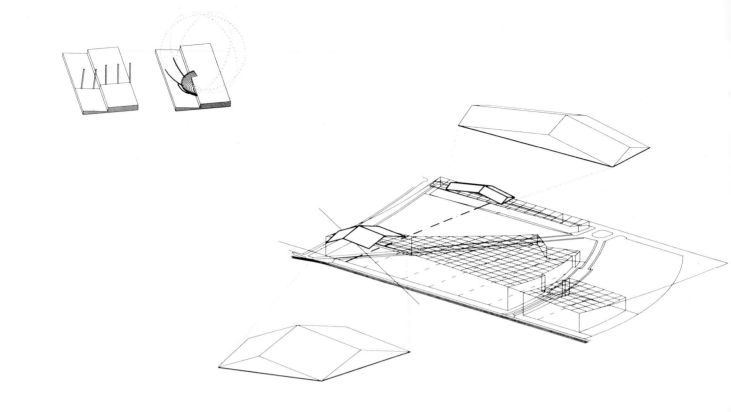

The next callig is a curved line, the move that joins critical destination points on the site. The points determine the path; the path determines the points. This is a horizontal walkway and the curves sometimes instigate excavations. On site, one curved line becomes the circumference of a spherical cut in the earth that leads to the subway. A landscape condition, a paved walk, and a movement system. The curve correlates built form with land form. If the land slopes, the buildings sitting on top are perpendicular to that tilted ground plane.

The idio-Descartes callig provides a number of organizational points and lines perpendicular to the ground on which it sits. Idio-Descartes is an intentional oxymoron, "idio" meaning idiosyncratic, and "Descartes" alleging a generic order.

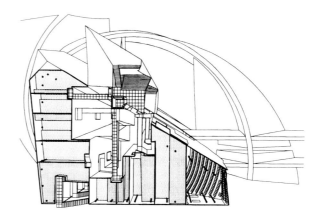

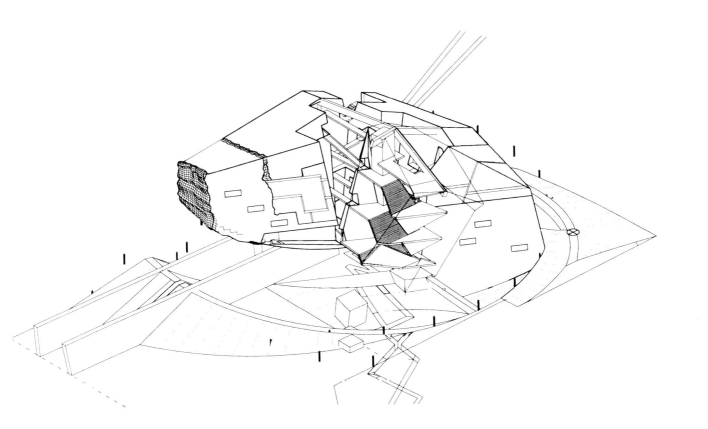

I designed a lid callig, a conceptual roof, as an analogue to the city's height limits. Theoretically it covers all seven sites. The roof makes a shape and a space—the how-high callig.

The ricochet, as it moves vertically, works its way up the wall on the second building site. Look at the building and you read its presence. It carves a circulation zone. The tree callig, the protected garden, the lid on the site, and the idio-Descartes curves impose their orders (with my help) on the two generic apartment blocks, describing the shapes without bothering about what's in the buildings.

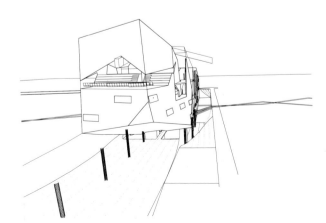

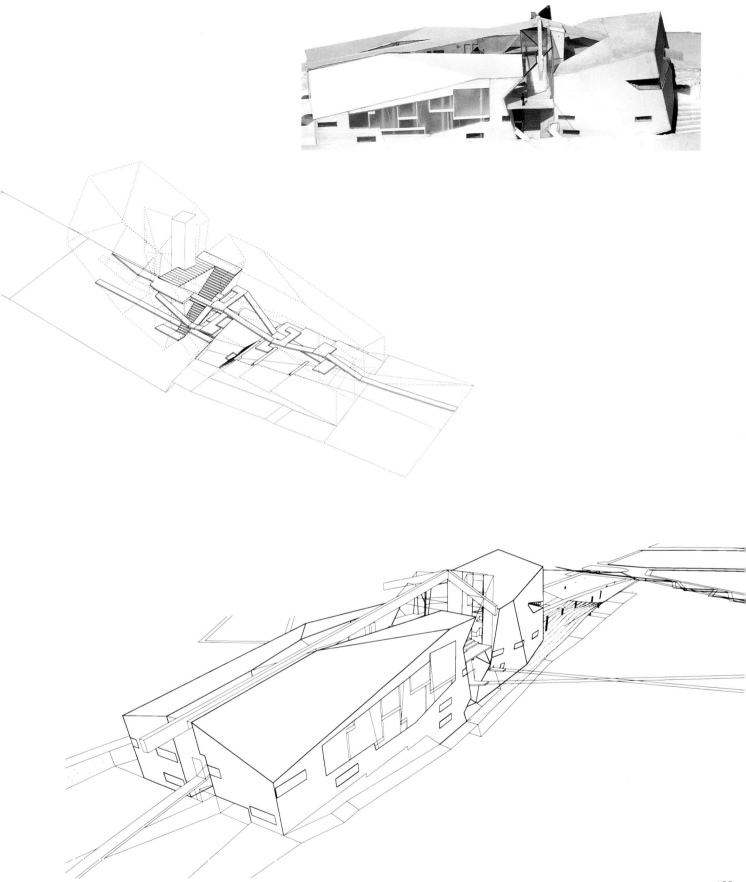

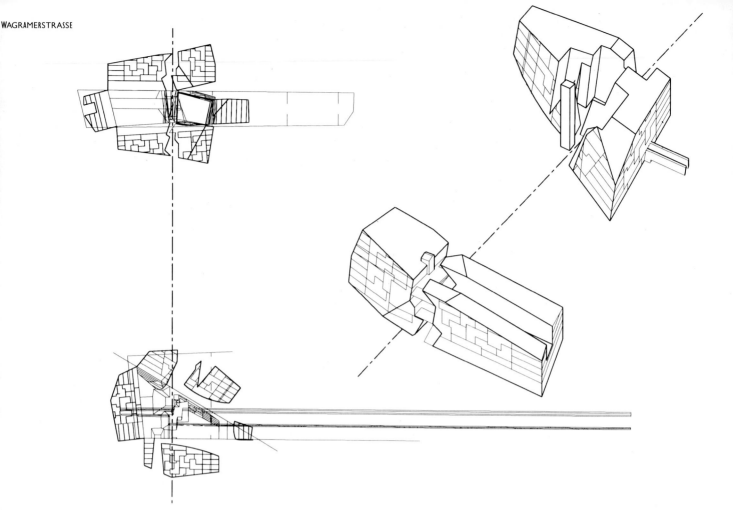

Another brick in the wall, courtesy of Pink Floyd, defines the assembly of units. Either the entire building block is a brick, or the units are irregular, mortarless bricks in the wall. An appeal to a bigger order, and a mechanism for construction without a conventional floor system.

There's a theoretical property line separating my site and the adjacent property. The joint occurs at the property line.

Jumping the property line is the origin of the bubble gum callig. It's not cosmological, but it can stretch and stick, so I can stick one built piece to another. The bubble gum works its way underneath to become a soffit, and finally inside as the acoustic liner for a cinema. The gum also got stuck to a stair.

Originally the bubble gum existed up high—an image of sky, a cloudy day holding a stair. Whether the bubble gum callig delivers a cosmological sky I won't say. But it might just stick the whole world together.

VIENNESE AUTHORITIES WERE SURPRISED

TO HEAR OF BUBBLE GUM AS A CRITERION

FOR CITY PLANNING.

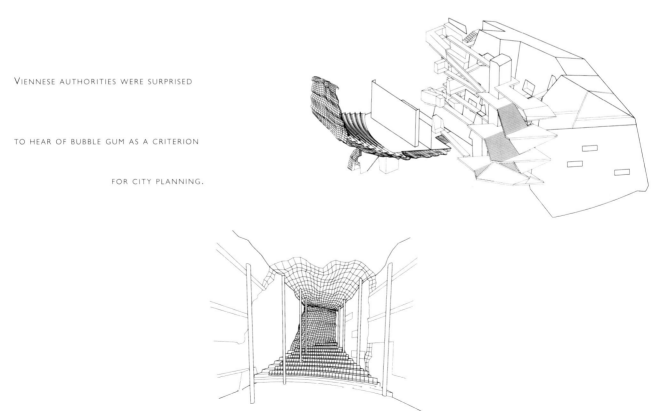

THE THEORETICAL SHADOWS
(NOT ACTUAL, BECAUSE SURROUNDING BUILDINGS
PRECLUDE THEIR LITERAL APPEARANCE)

MANIFEST THE NECESSITY OF THE PRESENCE OF EARTH, SUN, AND SKY IN THE LIFE OF A CITY

AS WELL AS AN INABILITY TO DELIVER THESE ELEMENTAL CONDITIONS UNAMBIGUOUSLY.

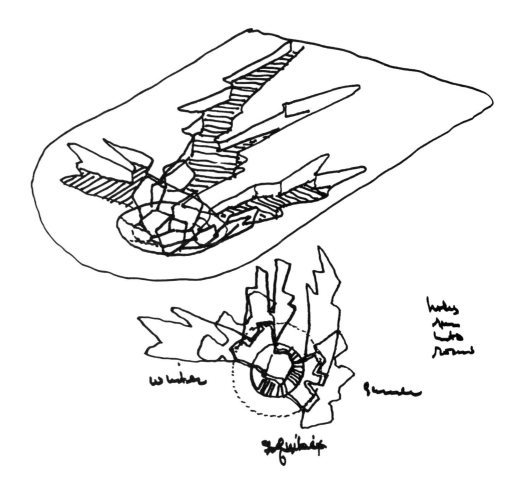

The project is an open-air amphitheater-in-the-round with an outdoor projection platform and large video screens. The facility can be used like Hyde Park, as a forum where purveyors of current wisdom(s) stand up and yell. Below the outdoor stage is an enclosed backstage accessed by two stairs, one on either side of the stage. Two large spaces below grade adjoin the staging area, with roofs formed by the bleachers above.

Pedestrians access the below-grade area by descending gradually on walks and stairs through two excavated slots. The first of these slots extends the line of Vesey Street to the west; the second extends to the north, anticipating pedestrian traffic from a proposed new office complex. A third axial line runs diagonally from north-northeast, extending a proposed walk

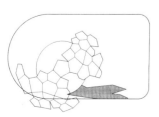

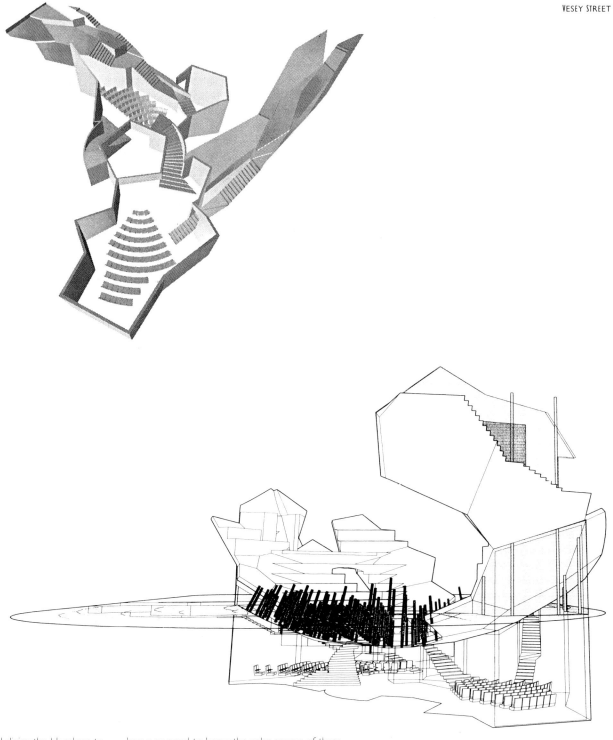

from the adjacent site and slicing the bleachers to provide access to the outdoor seating.

The source of the plan form of the two excavations is the shadows cast by the bleachers, oriented east-west at noon at the winter solstice and north-south at 6:00 pm at the summer solstice. The conceptual intention of the shadow projection is not to recall the Druids or to resurrect Stonehenge, and it's unlikely that park users would know or need to know the solar source of these cuts. The slots may remain enigmatic, but they are fun to play in.

205

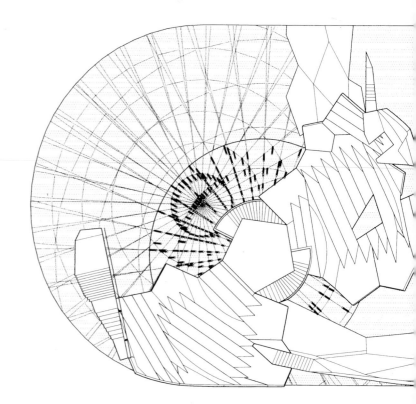

Formally, the theater involves the intersection of a partial sphere with an analogous sphere made of five-sided concrete plates that hold the bleacher seats. The two spheres have different geometric centers, both of which are distinct from the plan center of the turnaround curve. There is a literal and figurative jostling of centers without a simple geometric (or philosophical) resolution. A fundamental geometric order of sphere and pentasphere exists, but the interworkings of the theater seating, stage, projection screen, and solstice slots obviate a clear reading. The order's there; it's just difficult to locate.

A portion of the sphere is excavated adjacent to the five-sided outdoor stage and planted with grass, as is the entire site beyond the theater and slots. A series of analogous latitude and longitude lines that describe the underlying organizational orders of the two spheres and their centers is scraped onto the surface of the partial sphere and extends to the turnaround curve. At points where the lines intersect, 5'6"-high steel pipes placed perpendicular to the bowl's curving surface demarcate the scraped earth lines in the grass.

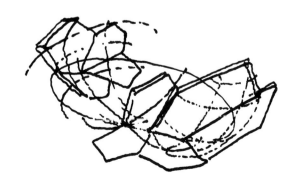

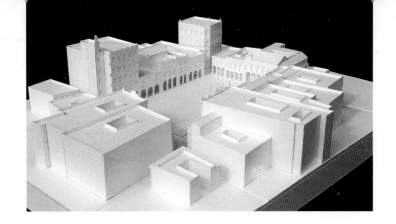

The Plaza Vieja is the erogenous zone of historic Havana. To alter the plaza, to redesign the space, is to advocate revitalizing architecture and city planning strategies in Cuba. Ergo: Attack the old plaza.

The proposal imposes a forum-theater-stadium—a multipurpose arena—on the deteriorating plaza, which has served various public purposes—as a park, market square, and carnival arena. The site remains a place for public gatherings. The existing colonial architecture will be substantially erased, leaving only residual images.

The new project confirms the plaza's tradition of redefinition and is consistent with both a history of architectural change and a continuity of purpose.

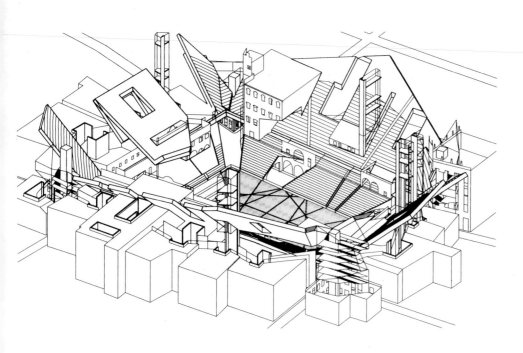

THE PROJECT INTENDS TO BE HISTORICALLY NAIVE.

IT ASSUMES THE WORLD CAN BECOME SOMETHING IT'S NOT.

DOESN'T ASSUME THAT WE KNOW THE CITY, THAT THE CITY KNOWS US,

THAT WE MERELY RESHUFFLE RECOGNIZABLE PIECES.

209

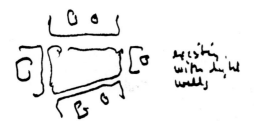

existing
with light
wells

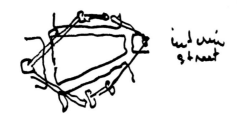

interior
street

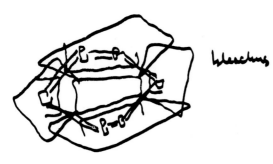

bleachers

The buildings around the plaza are three to six stories with enormous interior light wells, and are contained by the old Havana grid. The project ruptures that grid, dissolves a portion of it, and forms a more freely organized walk-street that cuts and removes portions of old structures, connecting and converting the light wells around the plaza. The ex-light wells are now public gathering points along a street that doesn't belong to the grid.

The new architecture intervenes in an old neighborhood, leaving a physical skeleton but implying a new social prospect. City buildings cut new bleachers. Bleachers slice old buildings, and the severed remains need to find new social purpose. Space is now defined above, below, or through the bleacher plane. And the new dissolve-the-block street makes exterior facades along what was once a dark interior archeology of old colonial buildings.

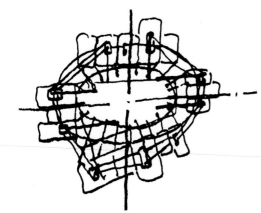

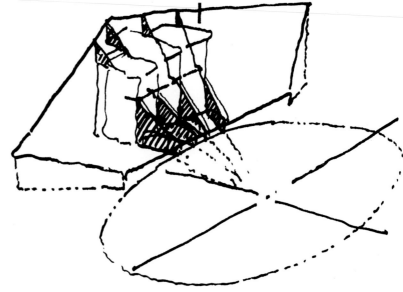

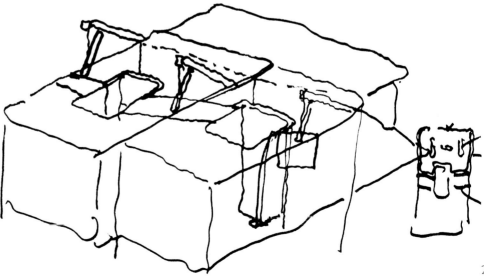

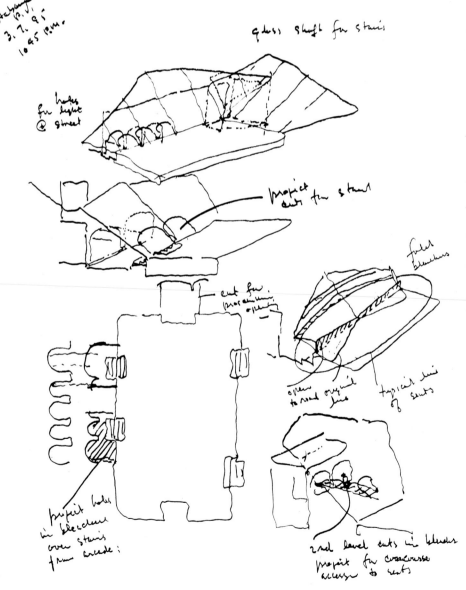

At the center of the north end of the old plaza arcade an existing building will become a stage with a new proscenium structure bent over the original roof. A new orchestra pit will be cut from the roof of the below-grade garage and positioned just south of the stage. Performances can occur on the stage or anywhere else in the plaza.

THE PROJECT DOESN'T SIMPLY BULLDOZE,

BUT IT'S NOT AFRAID TO BULLDOZE.

THE PROJECT LOOKS ASKANCE

AT THE BLOODLESS COLONIAL ARCHITECTURE,

BUT DOESN'T DENY IT A RESIDUAL PLACE.

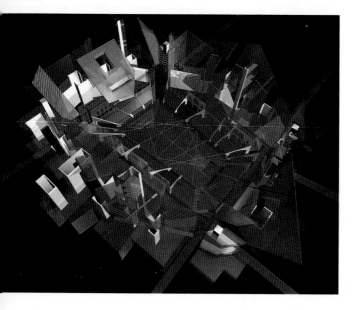

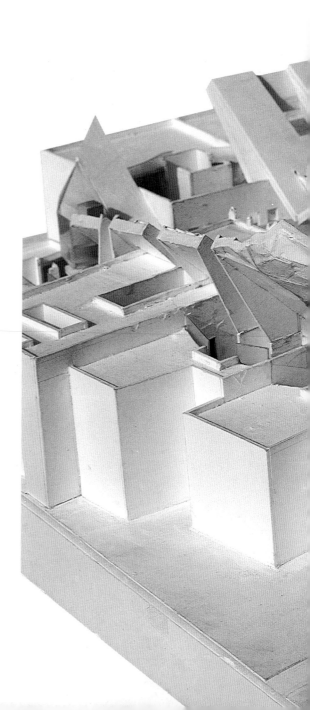

The intervention chases an intricate, not altogether legible relationship between old and new: How to make the old new? The arena bowl is set in the plaza. Sometimes the plaza gives way. Sometimes the bowl gives way. So the intervention is a hybrid, moving forward and backward in time.

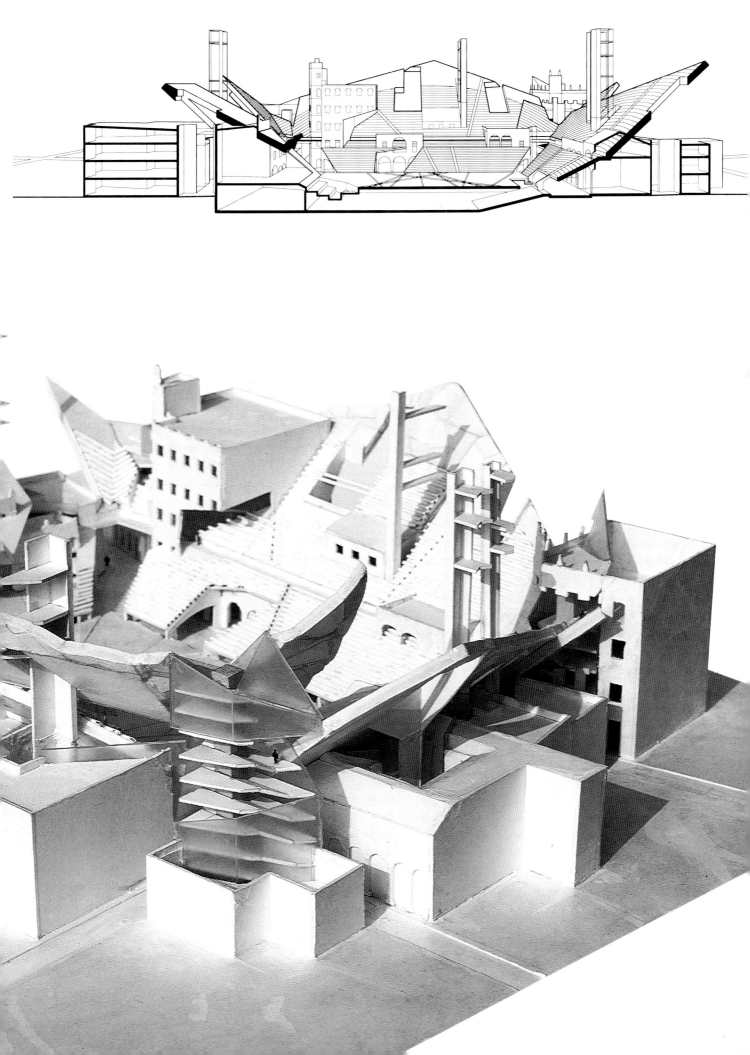

PROJECT CHRONOLOGY

SMALL TYPE INDICATES PROJECTS NOT DISCUSSED IN THIS VOLUME

1974–76 TRIPLEX APARTMENTS	PLAYA DEL REY, CALIFORNIA	1986–90 8522 NATIONAL BOULEVARD	CULVER CITY, CALIFORNIA
1977–78 COBB RESIDENCE	HOLLYWOOD, CALIFORNIA	1987– INCE COMPLEX	CULVER CITY, CALIFORNIA
1977–79 MORGENSTERN WAREHOUSE	LOS ANGELES, CALIFORNIA	1987–89 LINDBLADE TOWER	CULVER CITY, CALIFORNIA
1978–79 LA FAILLE HOUSE	MALIBU, CALIFORNIA	1987–89 PARAMOUNT LAUNDRY	CULVER CITY, CALIFORNIA
1979–80 GIBRALTAR SAVINGS AND LOAN	LOS ANGELES, CALIFORNIA	1988– T & L HOUSE	CULVER CITY, CALIFORNIA
1979–81 FIVE CONDOMINIUMS	PASADENA, CALIFORNIA	1988– 8522 NATIONAL OFFICE COMPLEX	CULVER CITY, CALIFORNIA
1979–82 708 HOUSE	LOS ANGELES, CALIFORNIA	1988 MULTI–UNIT HOUSING, MUSEUM OF CONTEMPORARY ART	LOS ANGELES, CALIFORNIA
1980 CHICAGO TRIBUNE TOWER	CHICAGO, ILLINOIS	1988–90 HYBRID ARTS	CULVER CITY, CALIFORNIA
1980 FUN HOUSE	HIDDEN VALLEY, CALIFORNIA	1988–90 QUALITATIVE RESEARCH CENTER	CULVER CITY, CALIFORNIA
1980–82 ADAMS HOUSE	HOLLYWOOD, CALIFORNIA	1988–90 GOALEN GROUP	CULVER CITY, CALIFORNIA
1980–82 LOGIN HOUSE	MALIBU, CALIFORNIA	1988–90 SCOTT MEDNICK AND ASSOCIATES	CULVER CITY, CALIFORNIA
1980–84 PIN BALL HOUSE	LOS ANGELES, CALIFORNIA	1988–90 GARY GROUP	CULVER CITY, CALIFORNIA
1981–82 HOUSES X AND Y	MALIBU, CALIFORNIA	1988–93 LAWSON/WESTEN HOUSE	BRENTWOOD, CALIFORNIA
1982 OFFICE BUILDING	COSTA MESA, CALIFORNIA	1989– SANDPIPER BRIDGE	CULVER CITY, CALIFORNIA
1982–84 PETAL HOUSE	WEST LOS ANGELES, CALIFORNIA	1989– WEDGEWOOD HOLLY COMPLEX	CULVER CITY, CALIFORNIA
1982–84 PIONEER COMMERCIAL CENTER	ARTESIA, CALIFORNIA	1989–95 SAMITAUR	LOS ANGELES, CALIFORNIA
1983–85 WORLD SAVINGS AND LOAN	LOS ANGELES, CALIFORNIA	1990– SPARCITY	CULVER CITY/LOS ANGELES, CALIFORNIA
1984–86 HONEY SPRINGS COUNTRY CLUB	SAN DIEGO COUNTY, CALIFORNIA	1990– WARNER THEATER	CULVER CITY, CALIFORNIA
1985 ESCONDIDO CIVIC CENTER	ESCONDIDO, CALIFORNIA	1990–94 BOX	CULVER CITY, CALIFORNIA
1985 LOWER EAST SIDE HOUSING/ INDIGENT PAVILION	NEW YORK, NEW YORK	1991– ARONOFF HOUSE	TARZANA, CALIFORNIA
1985 STACKED HOUSE	LOS ANGELES, CALIFORNIA	1991– HAYDEN TOWER	CULVER CITY, CALIFORNIA
1985 RESERVOIR HOUSE	LOS ANGELES, CALIFORNIA	1991 NARA CONVENTION CENTER	NARA, JAPAN
1986 SAN FRANCISCO STADIUM	SAN FRANCISCO, CALIFORNIA	1991 M-A-K (AUSTRIAN MUSEUM FOR APPLIED ARTS)	VIENNA, AUSTRIA
1986–87 YOKO UEHARA HOUSE	PASADENA, CALIFORNIA	1991–94 R I	CULVER CITY, CALIFORNIA
1986–87 TOKYO OPERA HOUSE	TOKYO, JAPAN		
1986–89 CENTRAL HOUSING OFFICE UNIVERSITY OF CALIFORNIA AT IRVINE	IRVINE, CALIFORNIA		

1991–95
METAFOR CULVER CITY, CALIFORNIA

1992–
STEALTH CULVER CITY, CALIFORNIA

1992–
IBIZA PASEO IBIZA, SPAIN

1992–
SAMITAUR 2 LOS ANGELES, CALIFORNIA

1993–
VLA SUN DRAWING PROJECT SANTA FE, NEW MEXICO

1993–
SANTA MONICA SCIENCE CENTER SANTA MONICA, CALIFORNIA

1993–
INCE THEATER CULVER CITY, CALIFORNIA

1993
R2 CULVER CITY, CALIFORNIA

1993
CONTEMPORARY ART CENTER TOURS, FRANCE

1993–94
IRS CULVER CITY, CALIFORNIA

1994
R3 THEATER CULVER CITY, CALIFORNIA

1994–
8520 ANNEX CULVER CITY, CALIFORNIA

1994–
PSF CULVER CITY, CALIFORNIA

1994–
BEEHIVE CULVER CITY, CALIFORNIA

1994–
WAGRAMERSTRASSE VIENNA, AUSTRIA

1994–
SAMITAUR 3 LOS ANGELES, CALIFORNIA

1994–
PLAZA VIEJA HAVANA, CUBA

1994–
VESEY STREET BATTERY PARK CITY, NEW YORK

1995–
LA CITY BRIDGE LOS ANGELES, CALIFORNIA

1995–
GASOMETER D-1 VIENNA, AUSTRIA

1995–
GREEN UMBRELLA CULVER CITY, CALIFORNIA

1995

Adria, Miguel. *Arquitectura* (Mexico), August/September, 1995, cover, pp. 52–65.
(STEALTH, WAGRAMERSTRASSE, VESEY STREET)

Chen, John. *Architectural Color Renderings.* New York: McGraw-Hill (forthcoming).
(GASOMETER D-1, VESEY STREET)

Cohen, Preston Scott, and Brooke Hodge, eds. *Eric Owen Moss: The Box.* New York: Princeton Architectural Press and Harvard University Graduate School of Design, (forthcoming).

"Conjunctive Points," *L'Arca,* special AIA Convention issue, April, 1995, cover, pp. 10–23.
(INCE COMPLEX, SAMITAUR, HAYDEN TRACT)

Connexux Visual Communication. *The New American House: Innovations in Residential Design and Construction. 30 Case Studies.* New York: Whitney Library of Design, 1995, pp. 40–51.
(LAWSON/WESTEN HOUSE)

Diamond, Richard. *North American Architecture Since the Kennedy Era* (forthcoming).
(PARAMOUNT LAUNDRY AND CENTRAL HOUSING OFFICE)

Dixon, John Morris. "Process: Superstructure," *Progressive Architecture,* July, 1995, pp. 60–69.
(SAMITAUR)

———. "The Santa Monica School: What's Its Lasting Contribution?" *Progressive Architecture,* May, 1995, cover, pp. 64–65, 67–70, 112, 114.

Dollens, Dennis L., ed. *Sites Architecture 26,* pp. 2–11.
(BOX)

"The 42nd Annual P/A Awards," *Progressive Architecture,* January, 1995, pp. 104–105, 111.
(INCE THEATER)

Fuchigami, Yuki. *50 World Architect.s.* Japan: Architectural Journalist Synectics, Inc. (forthcoming).

GA Document 43: GA International 95, May, 1995, pp. 78–83.
(INCE THEATER)

Garcia-Marques, Francesca. *L'Arca Plus 05: Monographie on Architecture 05,* 1995, pp. 94–97.
(ARONOFF HOUSE)

Greaves, Katy, ed. "Design Abroad: Skewed Geometries from Eric Owen Moss," *Hinge* magazine, May, 1995, pp. 38–40.
(LAWSON/WESTEN HOUSE)

Korean Architects, special 10th anniversary issue, April, 1995, cover, pp. 6–41.
(BOX, IRS, INCE THEATER, STEALTH)

Lee, Rendow. *Architectural Drawing Techniques* (forthcoming).
(LAWSON/WESTEN HOUSE, 8522 NATIONAL)

Moss, Eric Owen. "Brother Can You Spare A (para) Digm?" *L'Arca,* special AIA Convention issue, April, 1995, cover, p. 3.

Newman, Morris. "Who Should Get That Coveted One Percent?" *Progressive Architecture,* February, 1995, pp. 49–50.

Ryan, Raymund. "Rapturous Ruptures," *Architectural Review,* January, 1995, pp. 66–71.
(BOX, IRS)

Steele, James, *Lawson/Westen House.* Architecture in Detail and Technology (ADT) series. London: Phaidon Press, 1995.

Uddin, Muhammad. *Composite Drawing.* New York: McGraw-Hill (forthcoming).
(DRAWINGS OF LINDBLADE TOWER, LOWER EAST SIDE HOUSING, LAWSON/WESTEN HOUSE, NARA CONVENTION CENTER, STEALTH, INCE THEATER, IBIZA PASEO)

Vallée, Sheila. *L'Architecture du Futur.* Paris: Terrail (forthcoming).
(BOX, SAMITAUR)

Webb, Michael. "City of Angles," *Blueprint,* December–January, 1995, pp. 72–74.
(BOX, IRS)

1994

a+u, special issue, "Eric Owen Moss 1974–1994," November, 1994.

Anderton, Frances. "LA's Brand New Day," *Perspectives,* November, 1994, pp. 24–29.
(PARAMOUNT LAUNDRY, 8522 NATIONAL, BOX, IRS)

Antonelli, Paola. "Gioco Vorticista," *Abitare,* January, 1994, pp. 36–43.
(LAWSON/WESTEN HOUSE)

Betsky, Aaron. "Kantorencomplex National Boulevard," *de Architect,* September, 1994, pp. 85–89.
(8522 NATIONAL, HAYDEN TRACT)

———. "Post Industrial Encounters," *Architectural Record,* Record Interiors, September, 1994, pp. 68–73.
(BOX, IRS)

"Conference: Eric Owen Moss," *Arch & Life* (Germany), July/August, 1994, p. 38.
(LAWSON/WESTEN HOUSE)

"Designer's Diary: The Box," *Insite* (Toronto), November, 1994, pp. 18–19.
(BOX)

Dibar, Carlos. "En Los Angeles, altares domesticos," *Arquitectura,* supplement to *La Nacion* (Buenos Aires), March 30, 1994.
(LAWSON/WESTEN HOUSE)

Dietsch, Deborah. "Percent for Architecture," *Architecture,* July, 1994, p. 15.

"Eric Owen Moss Maison à Los Angeles," *L'Architecture d'Aujourd'hui,* April 15, 1994, pp. 74–77.
(LAWSON/WESTEN HOUSE)

Fonds Regional d'Art Contemporain. *L'Objet de l'Architecture: un état de la collection du FRAC Centre.* Bordeaux, France: Fonds Regional d'Art Contemporain, 1994.
(EXHIBITION CATALOGUE: ARONOFF HOUSE)

GA Houses, Projects 1994, April, 1994, pp. 110–111.
(R2)

Garcia-Marques, Francesca. "La Cubosfera," *L'Arca,* special houses issue, November, 1994, pp. 8–12.
(ARONOFF HOUSE)

Giovannini, Joseph. "Fresh Off the Drawing Board: An Innovative Design Activism Gives New Meaning to Cool in Culver City," *Los Angeles Times,* October 7, 1994, pp. 38–43, 50.
(CULVER CITY AND LOS ANGELES PROJECTS)

———. "LA Trouvée," *Zodiac,* special California issue, May, 1994, pp. 80, 250–257.
(SAMITAUR, STEALTH, GARY GROUP, LAWSON/WESTEN HOUSE)

Irace, Fulvio. "Los Angeles 1994: The Urban Landscape and Development: La Formazione di Un'Identita Architettonica," *Abitare,* May, 1994, pp. 214, 216.
(GARY GROUP)

Jodidio, Philip. "Les Architectes Californiens," *Connaissance des Arts,* October, 1994, cover, pp. 5, 107, 130–139.
(LAWSON/WESTEN HOUSE, HAYDEN TRACT, SAMITAUR, INCE COMPLEX)

Kalach, Alberto. "El Arquitecto Artifice, Eric Owen Moss," *Arquitectura* (Mexico), August, 1994, pp. 48–55.
(LAWSON/WESTEN HOUSE)

Merkel, Jane. "Architecture of Dislocation: The L.A. School," *Art in America*, February, 1994, pp. 33–38.
(REVIEW OF RIZZOLI MONOGRAPH, PARAMOUNT LAUNDRY, LINDBLADE TOWER, GARY GROUP)

Miller, Hillary, and Joycelyn Chi Fawaz. "Architecture and Art," *Traveler's Journal: Los Angeles, Insight for the Discriminating*, fall, 1994, p. 21.

Moss, Eric Owen. Interview by Kitty Felde, *National Public Radio*, August 10, 1994.
(1% FOR ART TAX)

———. "Pieces of Eight," *Simultaneous Landscapes: Journal of the Alaska Design Forum.* Vol. 3, Fall, 1994, pp. 2–9.

———. "Pieces of Eight," *Umriss* (Vienna), July, 1994, pp. 37–39.

———. "2 Rhino," in *The Architect's Dream: Houses for the Next Millennium.* Cincinnati, Ohio: The Contemporary Arts Center, 1994, pp. 40–43.
(EXHIBITION CATALOGUE: R2)

Muschamp, Herbert. "Rude Awakening," *New York Times*, January 23, 1994, The Week in Review.
(BOX)

Puzey, Dennis. "Living Sculpture," *House and Garden* (England), April, 1994, pp. 134–139.
(LAWSON/WESTEN HOUSE)

Steele, James. *Architecture in Process.* London: Academy Group, 1994, pp. 6, 112–141.
(VLA, SANTA MONICA SCIENCE CENTER, NARA CONVENTION CENTER)

———. *World Cities: Los Angeles.* London: Academy Group, 1994, pp. 92–107, 198–215, 248–253, 356, 357, 378–381.
(HAYDEN TRACT, HAYDEN TOWER, SPARCITY, SAMITAUR, INCE COMPLEX, GARY GROUP, PARAMOUNT LAUNDRY, LINDBLADE TOWER, 8522 NATIONAL, LAWSON/WESTEN HOUSE, SMSC, ARONOFF HOUSE)

Stein, Karen, and Aaron Betsky. "Urban Renewal," *Architectural Record*, July, 1994, pp. 62–69.
(INCE COMPLEX, SAMITAUR, HAYDEN TRACT, SPARCITY)

Vogel, Carol. "Inside Art," *New York Times*, April 1, 1994. The Living Arts.

Zevon, Susan. "Beaming Up Comfort," *House Beautiful*, September, 1994, pp. 104–109.
(LAWSON/WESTEN HOUSE)

1993

Betsky, Aaron. "In the Petal House, Construction Materials Come Into Full Flower," *Los Angeles Times*, March 11, 1993, Westside Section, p. J2.

"Colpi di Grazia a Culver City," *Lotus 77*, August, 1993, cover, pp. 92–105.
(INCE COMPLEX)

"Eric Moss: Made in the USA," *Magazine Neuf/Nieuw* (Belgium), Architecture & Design, June, 1993, pp. 17–28.
(INCE COMPLEX, 8522 NATIONAL)

"Eric Owen Moss: Lawson/Westen House," *a+u*, September, 1993, pp. 36–55.
(LAWSON/WESTEN HOUSE)

Freiman, Ziva. "Into the Uncharted," *Progressive Architecture*, May 1993, pp. 67–77.
(LAWSON/WESTEN HOUSE)

GA Houses 37, March, 1993, pp. 94–97.
(IBIZA PASEO)

GA Houses 38, July, 1993, pp. 78–97.
(LAWSON/WESTEN HOUSE)

Giovannini, Joseph. "Room at the Top," *Los Angeles Times Magazine*, April 25, 1993, pp. 34–37.
(LAWSON/WESTEN HOUSE)

Iovine, Julie. "A Space Odyssey," *New York Times Magazine*, November 1993, pp. 66–69.
(LAWSON/WESTEN HOUSE)

Jencks, Charles. *Heteropolis: Los Angeles, The Riots and the Strange Beauty of Hetero-Architecture.* London: Academy Group, 1993, pp. 20, 62–63, 106.
(PARAMOUNT LAUNDRY, LINDBLADE TOWER, GARY GROUP, LAWSON/WESTEN HOUSE, YOKO UEHARA HOUSE, 708 HOUSE, SPARCITY)

Jodidio, Philip, ed. *Contemporary American Architects Vol I.* Cologne: Benedikt Taschen Verlag, 1993, pp. 122–129.
(8522 NATIONAL, SMA, LAWSON/WESTEN HOUSE, STEALTH, NARA CONVENTION CENTER, GARY GROUP, ARONOFF HOUSE)

Knauf, Brigitte. "Bad Boy Gewinnt Neue Freunds," *Ambiente*, November, 1993, pp. 28–35.
(LAWSON/WESTEN HOUSE)

LeBlanc, Sydney. *Whitney Guide to 20th Century Architecture: 200 Key Buildings.* New York: Whitney Library of Design, 1993, p. 195.
(GARY GROUP, PARAMOUNT LAUNDRY, LINDBLADE TOWER, 8522 NATIONAL)

Lorenzelli, Tiziana. "Eric Owen Moss: Sottile umorismo, ironia, provocazione nei mobili dell'architetto californiano," *Ottagano*, April, 1993, pp. 45–52.
(FURNITURE)

Moss, Eric Owen. Interview, *KCOP Channel 13 News/Los Angeles*, May 21, 1993.

———. "Out of Place is the One Right Place," in *The End of Architecture: Documents and Manifestos: Vienna Architecture Conference.* Munich: Prestel Verlag, 1993, pp. 60–71, 99–134.
(GARY GROUP, SPARCITY, 8522 NATIONAL, SAMITAUR, NARA CONVENTION CENTER, ARONOFF HOUSE, MAK TERRACE PLATEAU, IRS, ROUNDTABLE DISCUSSION)

Muschamp, Herbert. "An Enterprise Zone for the Imagination," *New York Times*, March 14, 1993, p. 32.
(REVIEW OF EXHIBITION AT HARVARD UNIVERSITY GRADUATE SCHOOL OF DESIGN)

"Qué Verdad a Decir," *El arqa* (Uruguay), August, 1993, pp. 32–37.
(LAWSON/WESTEN HOUSE)

Sarzabal, Hernán Barbero. "Eric Owen Moss: Joyero de la chatarra," *El Cronista Arquitectura & Diseno* (Argentina), February 10, 1993, pp. 1–2, 8.
(PARAMOUNT LAUNDRY, LINDBLADE TOWER, GARY GROUP, ARONOFF HOUSE)

Steele, James. *Eric Owen Moss: Architectural Monograph No. 29.* London: Academy Group, 1993.
(CURRENT WORK)

———. *Los Angeles: The Contemporary Condition.* London: Phaidon Press, 1993, inside cover, pp. 62, 67, 69, 71, 85, 87, 154.
(MULTI-UNIT HOUSING PROJECT FOR MOCA, PETAL HOUSE, LAWSON/WESTEN HOUSE, PARAMOUNT LAUNDRY, LINDBLADE TOWER, GARY GROUP, 8522 NATIONAL)

"Wohnhaus in Los Angeles," *Baumeister*, September, 1993, pp. 35–39.
(LAWSON/WESTEN HOUSE)

1992

"Architektur + Asthetik: Amerika, Eric Owen Moss, Culver City, California," *Architektur Aktuell 148* (Austria), March, 1992, pp. 52–58.
(GARY GROUP, 8522 NATIONAL, SMA, GOALEN GROUP)

Bell, Judith. "Reshaping Architecture's Language," *World & I*, published by *The Washington Times*, April, 1992, pp. 178–183.
(CENTRAL HOUSING OFFICE, GARY GROUP, 8522 NATIONAL, VLA)

"Bürogebaüde in Culver City/Los Angeles," *Baumeister*, November, 1992, cover, pp. 14–21.
(GARY GROUP)

GA Houses 34, Projects 1992, March, 1992, pp. 74–75.
(ARONOFF HOUSE)

Giovannini, Joseph. "Gathering Moss," *Harper's Bazaar*, August, 1992, pp. 340–345, 398, 399.
(EOM PROFILE)

Kaplan, Sam Hall. "The Silly and the Sublime," *Buzz*, January/February, 1992, pp. 48, 50.
(PARAMOUNT LAUNDRY)

Lacy, Bill, and Susan DeMenil, eds. *Angels & Franciscans: Innovative Architecture From Los Angeles and San Francisco*. New York: Rizzoli International Publications, 1992, pp. 82–89.
(EXHIBITION CATALOGUE: SPARCITY, NARA CONVENTION CENTER)

"Mixed Media: Reclamation of the Building at 8522 National Boulevard," *Lotus 73*, August, 1992, cover, pp. 98–108.
(8522 NATIONAL)

Newman, Morris. "The Architectural Freedom of Eric Owen Moss," *Art in California*, July, 1992, pp. 20–21.
(EOM PROFILE)

Phillips, Allen. *Best in Office Interior Design*. London: Quarto Publications, 1992, pp. 198–221.
(PARAMOUNT LAUNDRY, LINDBLADE TOWER, GARY GROUP, GOALEN GROUP, SMA, QRC)

Ryan, Raymund. "Apocalypse Now," *Royal Institute of British Architects Journal*, March, 1992, pp. 38–41.

Slessor, Catherine. "Enigma Variations," *The Architectural Review*, September, 1992, pp. 24–29.
(8522 NATIONAL)

"The 39th Annual P/A Awards," *Progressive Architecture*, January, 1992, pp. 60, 62, 66, 68.
(SAMITAUR, ARONOFF HOUSE)

Toy, Maggie; Nicola Hodges; and Iona Spens, eds. *Theory & Experimentation: Architectural Ideas for Today and Tomorrow*. Architectural Design Profile No. 100. London: Academy Group, 1992, pp. 9–41.

Webb, Michael. "Eric Owen Moss designed a building for Frederick Smith who leased the site to Dick Gary and his Ad Agency," *Interior Architecture* (Australia), November/December, 1992, pp. 120–125.
(GARY GROUP)

World Space Design. Japan: NIC Ltd., Spring, 1992, pp. B-03042-X–B-03053-X.
(GOALEN GROUP, GARY GROUP, PARAMOUNT/LINDBLADE COMPLEX, 8522 NATIONAL)

1991

Bullivant, Lucy. *International Interiors 3*. London: Thames and Hudson, 1991, pp. 22–25.
(PARAMOUNT LAUNDRY, LINDBLADE TOWER)

Cohn, David. "Culver City Jazz: Eric Moss, del almacén al estucio," *Arquitectura Viva 21* (Spain), November/December, 1991, pp. 65–71.
(8522 NATIONAL, QRC, GOALEN GROUP)

Cook, Peter, and Rosie Llewellyn-Jones. *New Spirit in Architecture*. New York: Rizzoli International Publications, 1991, pp. 68–71.
(PETAL HOUSE, CENTRAL HOUSING OFFICE, LINDBLADE TOWER, PARAMOUNT LAUNDRY, 8522 NATIONAL)

Eric Owen Moss: Buildings and Projects. Preface by Philip Johnson, Introduction by Wolf Prix. New York: Rizzoli International Publications, 1991.

Freiman, Ziva. "Rites of Passage," *Progressive Architecture*, May, 1991, pp. 98–105.
(SMA, GOALEN GROUP)

"Los Ángeles: Oficios suburbanos, Tuberías de soporte: Lindblade Tower y Paramount Laundry, Culver City," *A & V Monograph 32* (Spain), Winter, 1991.
(PARAMOUNT LAUNDRY, LINDBLADE TOWER)

Russel, Beverly. "Questions and Answers," *Interiors Magazine*, January, 1991, pp. 120–121.
(QRC)

Stein, Karen, and Aaron Betsky. "Up Against the Wall," *Architectural Record*, March, 1991, pp. 106–113.
(GARY GROUP)

Thomsen, Christian W., "Chaos–Prinzip," *Ambiente*, June, 1991, pp. 71–77.
(8522 NATIONAL, SMA, QRC, PARAMOUNT LAUNDRY, LINDBLADE TOWER)

Webb, Michael. "The Re-Animators," *LA Style*, July, 1991, pp. 88–91.
(GARY GROUP, GOALEN GROUP, SMA)

1990

Art + Architecture + Society. Los Angeles: Frederick R. Weisman Art Foundation, 1990.
(SUMMARY OF WORKSHOP SPONSORED BY THE FREDERICK R. WEISMAN ART FOUNDATION, TORONTO, CANADA)

Betsky, Aaron. *Violated Perfection: Architecture and the Fragmentation of the Modern*. New York: Rizzoli International Publications, 1990, pp. 100–101.
(PARAMOUNT LAUNDRY, 8522 NATIONAL)

Boissiere, Olivier. *Eric Owen Moss Architecte. Lindblade Tower & Paramount Laundry: Reconversion à Culver City Californie, USA*. Paris: Architecture & Cie/Etat & Lieux, 1990.

———. "Eric Owen Moss: des architectures familieres et autonomes," *L'Architecture d'Aujourd'hui*, October, 1990, pp. 153–158.
(PARAMOUNT LAUNDRY, GARY GROUP, 8522 NATIONAL, QRC)

Dietsch, Deborah K. "Circumstantial Evidence," *Architecture*, June, 1990, pp. 90–95.
(QRC)

McDonnough, Michael. "An American Saga," *Metropolis*, March, 1990, pp. 40–41.
(PARAMOUNT LAUNDRY, 8522 NATIONAL)

"MoCA Housing Competition," *GA Houses 29*, July, 1990, pp. 20–21.

Moore, Rowan. "Complexity and Contradiction," *Blueprint*, May, 1990, pp. 41–43.
(INTERVIEW WITH EOM, LINDBLADE TOWER, PARAMOUNT LAUNDRY, 8522 NATIONAL)

Schindler House, Los Angeles, California, Exhibition of Havana projects, October, 1995

GA Gallery, Tokyo, Japan, "Eric Owen Moss," June 17–July 23, 1995

GA Gallery, Tokyo, Japan, "GA International, 1995," April, 1995

School of Architecture, Princeton University, Princeton, New Jersey, "Coughing Up the Moon: The Work of Eric Owen Moss," March 20–April 28, 1995

Österreichische Museum für Angewandte Kunst, Vienna, Austria, "MANIFESTOS– International Exhibition of Contemporary Architecture, Havana, Cuba," December 29, 1994–June, 1995

Contemporary Art Center, Tours, France, "Concours pour l'Amenagement du Site Francis Poulenc," (Contemporary Art Center competition), December, 1993

The Contemporary Arts Center, Cincinnati, Ohio, "The Architect's Dream: Houses of the Next Millenium," (Rhino House), December, 1993

Philippe Uzzan Galerie, Paris, France, "The Great Square Has No Corners," (Fun House and Lawson/Westen House), September 11– November 27, 1993

Fonds Regional d'Art Contemporain du Centre (FRAC), Bordeaux, France, July 9–September 5, 1993

Aspen Art Museum, Aspen, Colorado, "Models, Drawings, Furniture: Eric Owen Moss," June 3–July 4, 1993

Harvard University Graduate School of Design, Cambridge, Massachusetts, "Schizophrenia is a Cure, Not a Disease," Spring, 1993

Santa Monica Museum of Art, Santa Monica, California, "Angels & Franciscans: Innovative Architecture from Los Angeles and San Francisco," February 7–March, 1993

Museum für Gestaltung, Zurich, Switzerland, "New Realities–Neue Wirklichkeiten II: Architektur–Animationen–Installationen," January 27–April 4, 1993

Touring exhibition, Washington, D.C.; New York; Toronto; Denver; San Francisco; Los Angeles, Progressive Architecture, "New Public Realm," (solutions from the competition), October 23, 1991– March 20, 1992

University of California at Los Angeles, Graduate School of Architecture, "Excavation," October 19–November 6, 1992

University of Zagreb, Zagreb, Croatia, "Houses in Los Angeles, California," Fall, 1992

Leo Castelli/Gagosian Gallery, New York, New York, "Angels & Franciscans: Innovative Architecture from Los Angeles and San Francisco," September 26– November 7, 1992

GA Gallery, Toyko, Japan, "Contemporary Architectural Freehand Drawing," September 12–October 18, 1992

Royal Academy of Arts, London, England, "Theory & Experimentation," June 9– June 23, 1992

Gallery of Functional Art, Santa Monica, California, "Architects' Art 1992," February, 1992

Bartlett School of Architecture and Urban Design, London, England, "New Spirit in Architecture," November, 1991

Österreichische Museum für Angewandte Kunst, Vienna, Austria, "Terrassenplateau," July, 1991

Bryce Bannatyne Gallery, Santa Monica, California, "Conceptual Drawings by Architects," January 19–March 10, 1991

Salle des Tirages du Credit Foncier de France, Paris, France, "Olivier Boissiere and Les Editions du Demi-Cercle," June 27– July 13, 1990

Harvard University Graduate School of Design, Cambridge, Massachusetts, "Midnight at the Oasis," March 15–April 14, 1990

Museum of Contemporary Art, Los Angeles, California, "Blueprints for Modern Living: History and Legacy of the Case Study Houses," October 14, 1989– February 18, 1990

Sofia, Bulgaria, "World Biennale of Architecture– Interarch '89," June 20–26, 1989

St. Louis Museum of Art, St. Louis, Missouri, "National AIA Award Winners," May, 1989

Jacob K. Javits Convention Center, New York, New York, "National AIA Award Winners," May, 1988

National Academy of Design, New York, New York, "The Experimental Tradition: Twenty–five Years of American Architectural Competitions, 1960–1985," The Architectural League of New York, May–June, 1988

GA Gallery, Tokyo, Japan, "The Emerging Generation in USA," October, 1987

The Urban Center, New York, New York, "Emerging Voices," The Architectural League of New York, September, 1986

Harvard University Graduate School of Design, Cambridge, Massachusetts, "The Indigent as King," April 9–23, 1985

GA Gallery, Tokyo, Japan, "California Architecture: Eric Moss/Morphosis," April–June, 1985

The Architectural Association, London, England, "Los Angeles Now," April 2–May 21, 1983

La Jolla Museum of Contemporary Art, La Jolla, California, "The California Condition–A Pregnant Architecture," November 13, 1982–January 2, 1983

Paris, France, "Biennale de Paris: Section Architecture 1982, La modernité ou l'esprit du temps," August, 1982

The Architectural Gallery, Venice, California, "Selected Projects," November, 1979

1995

AIA National Honor Award

(CENTRAL HOUSING OFFICE,
UNIVERSITY OF CALIFORNIA AT IRVINE)

CC/AIA Design Honor Award

(BOX)

CC/AIA Design Honor Award

(LAWSON/WESTEN HOUSE)

DuPont Benedictus Award for Innovation in the
Architectural Use of Laminated Glass

(BOX)

Progressive Architecture Design Award

(INCE THEATER)

1994

LA/AIA Design Award

(BOX)

LA/AIA Design Award

(IRS)

AIA National Interior Design Award of Excellence

(LAWSON/WESTEN HOUSE)

LA/AIA Design Award

(LAWSON/WESTEN HOUSE)

1993

LA/AIA Design Award

(NARA CONVENTION CENTER)

1992

AIA National Interior Design Award of Excellence

(GARY GROUP)

AIA National Interior Design Award of Excellence

(8522 NATIONAL BOULEVARD)

Progressive Architecture Design Award

(SAMITAUR)

Progressive Architecture Design Award

(ARONOFF HOUSE)

1991

LA/AIA Honor Award

(SCOTT MEDNICK AND ASSOCIATES)

LA/AIA Honor Award

(GARY GROUP)

CC/AIA Urban Design/Adaptive Re-Use Award

(8522 NATIONAL OFFICE COMPLEX)

Interiors Design Award

(QUALITATIVE RESEARCH CENTER)

1990

LA/AIA Award

(PARAMOUNT LAUNDRY)

1989

AIA National Honor Award

(CENTRAL HOUSING OFFICE,
UNIVERSITY OF CALIFORNIA AT IRVINE)

1988

LA/AIA Award

(8522 NATIONAL BOULEVARD)

AIA National Honor Award

(8522 NATIONAL BOULEVARD)

CC/AIA Award

(8522 NATIONAL BOULEVARD)

1986

CC/AIA Award

(PETAL HOUSE)

1984

Architectural Record Award
"Award Winning Interiors"

(WORLD SAVINGS AND LOAN)

1983

LA/AIA Award

(FUN HOUSE)

LA/AIA Honor Award

(PETAL HOUSE)

1981

CC/AIA Award

(MORGENSTERN WAREHOUSE)

1979

LA/AIA Award

(MORGENSTERN WAREHOUSE)

1978

Progressive Architecture Design Award

(MORGENSTERN WAREHOUSE)

1977

LA/AIA Award

(PLAYA DEL REY TRIPLEX)

JAY VANOS

SCOTT NAKAO

THOMAS AHN		MATEI AGARICI	
GREG BAKER	JERRY SULLIVAN	KATHY AHN	HAO KO
JOHN BENCHER	ERIC STULTZ	RANYA ALOMAR	ANNE KOSMAL
ANN BERGREN	JANEK TABENCKI	ANDREAS AUG	EMILY KOVENER
ALAN BINN	JOSEPH TIU	MARCO BENJAMIN	CAHD KURZ
DANA SWINSKY CANTELMO	ELIZABETH TORBATI	LOREN BESWICK	HIROSHI KUWATA
TODD CONVERSANO	DAVID WICK	TED P. BRANDT	ANDERSON LEE
PETER DISABATINO		FRANK BRODBECK	MARK LEHMAN
JANEK TABENCKI DOMBROWA		MARLIES BRUESS	CHEEN LIN
ISABEL DUVIVIER		PEGGY BUNN	ANDREW LINDLEY
GEORGE ELIAN		STEPHANIE BUSCH	GRACE EN-LUI LU
AUGIS GEDGAUDAS		AMEDEE BUTT	CHRISTOPH LUEDER
PAUL GROH	ANNETTE BAGHDASARIAN	DAMONSIM CHATHURATTAPHOL	DANA MANSFIELD
MARK HARRIS	JESSICA BRONSON	TENG-CHIN CHEN	PHILIPPE MARMILLOD
TRISHA HARTDEN	ANA CHERTA	JOHN CHO	ROSE MEHRKHAH
SOPHIE HARVEY	TAMARA GOULD	SU-SHIEN CHO	FRANK MEYL
ERIC HOLMQUIST	NATALYA KARAVAY	ALFRED CHO	MOGENS MILBACH
CAROL HOVE	GABRIELLE KLUGER	LORENZA CRISTOFOLINI	ANA PAULA MOI
GEVIK HOVSEPIAN	KARIN MAHLE	DOMINGO CUEVAS	ANNE MOONEY
SHENG-YUAN HWANG	MARY EAVES MITCHEL	DANIEL DELGADO	KIRA OGLE
SCOTT HUNTER	MAUREEN MOSS	JOHN DE VERA	DOROTHY OTTOLIA
AMANDA HYDE	ERIC OTTO	EMIL DILANIAN	URS PADRUN
DENNIS IGE	RAYMOND RICORD	KISHANI DE SILVA	SUMATHI PONNAMBALAM
RANDY JACOBSEN		MALGORZATA KINGA DOROSZ	PHILLIP RA
SHARON JUDELMAN		INAKI EROSTARBE	ANDY RATZSCH
AUSTIN KELLY		JORGE V. SUSO FERNANDEZ-FIGARES	SUNNIE RHEE
CHRISTINE LAWSON		JUAN GARCIA	ERIC RICH
JAE LIM		JOSE GONZALES	SALLY RIGG
PAROS MAMIKUNIAN		DIANE GOURDAL	EDUOARDO SABATER
MAX MASSIE		VELVET HAMMERSCHMIDT	IDRIS SAMAD
LAWRENCE O'TOOLE		TRICIA HARDING	DARYUSCH SEPEHR
JOSE PIMENTEL		MUNAH HEDJAZI	CRAIG SHIMAHARA
MARK PRZEKOP		ANDREAS HEIPP	DARCI SHUNICK
JENNIFER RAKOW		VERONICA HINKLEY	CURT SIMMONS
LUCAS RIOS		MARK HUMPHREYS	JORGE SUSO
ELISSA SCRAFANO		KENNY HUO	DON THURSBY
NICK SEIRUP		KATHY ISHIKAWA	EVELYN TICKLE
NAOTO SEKIGUCHI		SUSANNE JENSEN	CHRIS WEGSCHEID
ELISABETH SPRINGFELDT		MATHIAS JOHANNSEN	SABINE WERNER
RAVINDRAN KODALUR SUBRAMANIAN		JOY KELLER	DAVID WILLIAMS
		TAE KIM	RICHARD YANCEY
		ANDREAS KIRBERG	HELEN YEE
			WARREN ANTHONY YOUNG

PHOTO CREDITS